The Pluralistic Therapy Primer

Kate Smith and
Ani de la Prida

First published in 2021

PCCS Books Ltd
Wyastone Business Park
Wyastone Leys
Monmouth
NP25 3SR
UK

Tel +44 (0)1600 891509
contact@pccs-books.co.uk
www.pccs-books.co.uk

© Kate Smith and Ani de la Prida, 2021
Foreword, © Mick Cooper, 2021
Introduction, © Pete Sanders, 2021

All rights reserved.
No part of this publication may be reproduced, stored in a retrieval system, transmitted or utilised in any form by any means, electronic, mechanical, photocopying or recording or otherwise without permission in writing from the publishers.

The authors have asserted their right to be identified as the authors of this work in accordance with the Copyright, Designs and Patents Act 1988.

The Pluralistic Therapy Primer

A CIP catalogue record for this book is available from the British Library.

ISBNs   paperback   978 1 910919 86 6
              epub   978 1 910919 87 3

Cover design by Jason Anscomb
Printed in the UK by 4edge, Essex

This product has been assessed as low risk and can be used safely without safety information.
Product code – 012025300
The manufacturer's authorised representative in the EU for product safety is:
Easy Access System Europe – Mustamäe tee 50, 10621 Tallinn, Estonia
gpsr.requests@easproject.com

Praise for *The Pluralistic Therapy Primer*

This book will likely be a core text in the counselling and psychotherapy literature. Trainee therapists will find here an overview of the approach to help them make sense of a range of inter-connected concepts and practices. Experienced practitioners who are curious about the pluralistic framework will find here a foundational text to help them explore the pluralistic territory and their place within it. Using case examples, rich detail and clear language, this primer prepares counsellors and psychotherapists for this abundantly varied and collaborative way of being with clients.
Nicola Blunden, Director of Studies, Metanoia Institute, London

This book is a very welcome addition to PCCS's Primer series. The authors write clearly and sensitively about pluralistic therapy, which is growing in popularity among counsellors and therapists who are not wedded to a particular way of working with clients. Of particular value is the chapter where the authors answer commonly asked questions concerning pluralistic therapy, and another that provides a composite case study. It is my hope that this book will bring pluralistic therapy to the attention of practitioners who seek a broad, inclusive framework to guide their therapeutic work and to trainers who are looking to train flexible and open-minded therapists. I highly recommend it .
Windy Dryden, Emeritus Professor of Psychotherapeutic Studies, Goldsmiths University of London

Kate Smith and Ani de la Prida have provided us with an essential tool for those interested in learning about how to apply a pluralistic perspective to their counselling and helping practice. Through their rich narrative and range of accessible chapters, they offer ways of weaving pluralistic thinking and practice skills into day-to-day counselling work. Their concept of a task taxonomy is a great way to convey central elements of working pluralistically, providing a novel tool for reviewing practice in training, supervision and research. In a nutshell, their primer prepares practitioners for pluralistic practice. It will be essential reading for the rapidly growing

international group of practitioners interested in developing a pluralistic perspective on practice.
Lynne Gabriel, Professor of Counselling and Mental Health, York St John University

This book celebrates the creativity and resourcefulness of clients and therapists and explains how they can draw on their combined knowledge and life experience to address problems in living. The authors combine philosophical and research-based sources, along with practical guidelines and a wealth of case examples, in a consistently readable and engaging manner. It is a book that is clear, profound and highly recommended.
John McLeod, Emeritus Professor of Counselling, Abertay University, and Visiting Professor, Institute for Integrative Psychotherapy and Counselling, Dublin

This primer offers an accessible and informative introduction to an approach to counselling and psychotherapy practice that emphasises the capacity of the client and therapist to work collaboratively together and share decisions about the direction and focus of therapy. It is essential reading for anyone interested in developing an understanding not only of pluralistic practice itself but also of the broader tradition of psychotherapy integration that it represents.
Julia McLeod, Lecturer in Counselling and Psychotherapy, Abertay University

The growing interesting in pluralistic practice has, perhaps, spoken to the understanding that people often need different things at different times in therapy. How we meet the diverse needs of people from diverse communities in a truly inclusive and collaborative way can be more of a challenge. Kate Smith and Ani de la Prida have, in this book, provided an erudite and engaging narrative about pluralism and pluralistic practice. This is, frankly, a superbly written text that provides the interested, the inquisitive and the experienced with a wonderful gateway into the world of pluralism.
Dr Andrew Reeves, Associate Professor in the Counselling Professions and Mental Health

Contents

	Foreword – *Mick Cooper*	*ix*
	Series introduction – *Pete Sanders*	*1*
1.	What is pluralistic therapy?	*7*
2.	Key principles	*13*
3.	Problems in living	*20*
4.	The collaborative relationship	*25*
5.	The process of pluralistic therapy	*39*
6.	The process of change	*59*
7.	Training, professional development and supervision	*64*
8.	Common questions and answers	*74*
9.	Research on pluralistic therapy	*81*
10.	Case study	*89*
	Appendix 1: Resources for learning	*103*
	Appendix 2: Cooper–Norcross Inventory of Preferences	*106*
	Glossary	*110*
	References	*113*
	Index	*124*

Dedication

Kate Smith
For my parents (without whom…)

Ani de la Prida
To my family, who always believe I can do anything.

Author biographies

Kate Smith qualified as a pluralistic therapist in 2009 and currently heads the Division of Health Sciences at Abertay University, the original home of pluralistic therapy training. Kate obtained her first and master's degrees at Cambridge University and went on to complete her doctoral research at the University of St Andrews, on the links between autobiographical memory, life stories and mental health. She is the author of numerous academic and practitioner publications on pluralism and mental health. She is a chartered psychologist, a founder member and chair of the Pluralistic Practitioner Network and co-chair of the International Conference on Pluralistic Counselling and Psychotherapy. She maintains a small practice, supervises pluralistic practitioners and is on the Board of Governors of the British Association for Counselling and Psychotherapy. Kate is the mother of two sons and lives in Scotland.

Ani de la Prida is a psychotherapist, creative arts counsellor and supervisor. She has 20 years' experience working with groups, adults, children and young people in a range of settings. She currently has a small private practice and is on the Executive Committee of the Private Practice division of the British Association for Counselling and Psychotherapy. Ani is a lecturer and teaches on the pluralistic counselling programme at the University of East London, where she did her master's degree research on the use of digital media in therapy. Ani is also the founder and course director of the Association for Person Centred Creative Arts. She is author of *What Works in Counselling and Psychotherapy Relationships* (BACP, 2020).

Acknowledgments

To my clients, to Julia McLeod, Mhairi Thurston, Marcia Stoll, Fiona Stirling, Lynne Thomas, and Sally Lumsdaine, and to the students at Abertay, who have taught me almost everything I know about pluralistic therapy (and to John, Mick and the Pluralistic Network for the other bits); to Catherine and the team at PCCS Books for your gracious patience throughout, and to Vincent, Gabe and Max for listening. Thank you.
Kate Smith

It takes a village… To Mick, for all your support and encouragement and for trusting that I could bring something of value to the pluralistic approach. To Catherine and the team at PCCS, for your support and guidance, which helped to shape this book. To Teresa and Dori, for planting strong seeds and nurturing my growth. And especially to my family: Chris, for the endless support and endless cups of coffee, and Jordan for introducing me to the wonders of Zotero and for all the midnight proofreading. Thank you.
Ani de la Prida

Foreword
Mick Cooper

What makes the pluralistic approach to therapy unique is that it starts with ethics. Other approaches, like person-centred or existential, have strong ethical dimensions and people often come into these approaches because they want to relate to clients in empowering and equalising ways. When the foundations of these approaches are articulated, however, it is often in terms of a particular model of the human being, or of what is most effective in therapy.

The pluralistic approach is different. Rather than starting with the question, 'How can we understand people?' or even, 'How can we best help our clients?', the pluralistic approach starts with the question, 'How can we relate to our clients in the most deeply respectful and valuing ways?' From here comes a range of understandings of people and a deep desire to help them change in ways that are helpful to them. But underpinning all of this is the commitment to being there *for* them. This is the core of the pluralistic approach, and it is essential to understand that grounding in order to really grasp what pluralism is about.

One of the first consequences of this ethical standpoint is that, as therapists, there's a commitment to trying to 'bracket' our assumptions and biases – so that we can be there for our clients as much as we can. In particular, this means putting to one side strong emotional allegiances to any one therapeutic approach or set of therapeutic methods. This doesn't mean denying it; it just means holding it lightly and being open to what else might be 'out there'. Because the reality, as the evidence shows, is that lots of different things can be helpful to different clients at different points in time. There's no one 'right' way of doing therapy; no evidence – to date – that any one particular orientation or method is superior to all the others.

When we start holding our own assumptions more lightly, we also then get more interested in what clients themselves think might help. That doesn't mean they will always know, or that they can always articulate it. But by creating a space in which that dialogue is possible, clients have the opportunity to bring their own wants, preferences and 'directions' into the therapeutic work – to make it their own.

Just to be clear, this is not about therapists being able to offer each and every method of intervention to clients. We all have our limits – what we are willing and able to offer – and having that dialogue with clients is about finding the meeting point(s) between what they want and what we're able to do. Again, it's back to dialogue, and that's back to relationality, and that's back to a deep and caring respect for the client and their way of being in the world – what the existential-relational philosopher Martin Buber termed an 'I-Thou' stance.

So a pluralistic approach to counselling and psychotherapy means a pluralism across orientations (that all therapies have something to offer), and a pluralism across clients (that different clients may benefit from different things at different points in time), and a pluralism across perspectives (that both client and therapist have something to offer to the process of therapy). And in recent years we've realised that there are other pluralisms that we should be embracing in our approach. For instance, there's a pluralism across cultures (an openness to the different frames, values and practices that a client might bring), and an 'internal' pluralism (the recognition that clients can have different voices 'inside' them, pulling, at times, in opposing directions).

What's been particularly exciting for me, as one of the first writers on this pluralistic approach, is to see new voices and perspectives coming into the field (a pluralism across pluralistic perspectives!). I feel it's been a real limitation, up to now, that so much of the pluralistic writing has come from my own perspective and that of John McLeod – both of us (apologies, John!) old white men.

So I'm so delighted that Kate and Ani have written this pluralistic primer, which has brought their fresh, new perspectives into the heart of the pluralistic field. It's a great book, partly because it gives a much-needed new summary of what pluralistic therapy is all about, but also because it introduces a range of new ideas and practices into the pluralistic 'canon'. For instance, the concept of 'relational stances', the use of creative methods in pluralistic therapy, and acknowledging the diversity within pluralism itself.

As highly experienced practitioners and trainers, Kate and Ani are the perfect guides to the pluralistic approach. The book takes you through the philosophical and ethical foundations of the approach before going on to present concrete, vivid, engaging descriptions of how it can be applied in practice. A final case study really shows the 'inner workings' of a pluralistic approach.

Pluralism, as Ani and Kate make clear throughout the book, is fundamentally about embracing and celebrating diversity. It's about taking all those things that make people special and unique and really prizing that. Pluralism is about the specialness of the client in front of us, and a commitment to working with this person, being alongside them in the journey that they want to go on, rather than taking them off on our trip. If you are interested in relating to clients in this way, and what it all means in practice, *The Pluralistic Therapy Primer* is a brilliant place to start. Enjoy!

Mick Cooper
Professor of Counselling Psychology, University of Roehampton

Series introduction
Pete Sanders

Counselling

Before we launch into pluralistic ways of working, it might be helpful to take a look at some definitions of counselling itself. It is important to locate the helping activity of counselling in relation to other helping activities in order to avoid confusion regarding the purpose of this book. This book is specifically aimed at people wanting to learn about pluralistic therapy, or counselling, with no previous experience or knowledge of counselling or psychology. The key word here is counselling.

So what do we mean by counselling?

What is counselling for?

One way of defining counselling is to look at what it is useful for. In the past 30 years, counselling has become ubiquitous, and it is perilously close to being presented as a panacea for just about everything. Some critics say that the emerging 'profession' of counselling has much to gain for claiming, on behalf of counsellors and therapists, that counselling is good for everything. It would be wrong to make such claims: counselling has its limits and part of being a counsellor is to know what those limits are. The problem is that when we are in distress, it is comforting to think that there is a simple answer around the corner.

The situation is not made any easier when we understand that simply sitting down and taking time out from a busy life can make things seem better. Counsellors must be able to explain to their clients the differences between this very important relief and comfort that can be gained from compassionate human contact on the one hand, and counselling as a specialist activity on the other. Counselling can help people in certain states of distress and usually involves change:

- change in the way the client sees things or themselves
- change in the way a client thinks about things or themselves
- change in the way a client feels about things or themselves
- change in the way a client behaves.

Although many people will not be able to put it neatly into a few words, what they seek from counselling can be roughly summarised in a few categories:

- support
- recovery
- problem-solving
- gaining insight or self-awareness
- developing new strategies for living.

The sort of distress that counselling can help is often called 'emotional' or 'psychological' and can include:

- stress – a very general and possibly over-used term, but there are some situations in life, especially those that you can't control, that might leave you feeling so stressed that it interferes with your everyday life
- conflict – at home or work
- bereavement – whether a relative or friend. Indeed, having anything permanently taken away might lead to a feeling of bereavement, such as losing your job or losing your ability to do something like walk, play sport or have sex

- depression – another over-used term and not one to be taken lightly. Many life events can make us feel low and talking it over really does help. The popular term 'depression' can cover everything from feeling understandably low after having your purse stolen or losing your job, through to being unable to get up in the morning or eat properly because you think life is not worth living
- coping with poor health – e.g. having a long-standing health problem or receiving a diagnosis of a serious or terminal illness
- trauma – e.g. surviving (including witnessing) something very disturbing (including abuse of various forms).

What counselling is not for

When someone decides to attend counselling sessions, they are usually, by definition, distressed. It is, therefore, particularly important that the client doesn't have either their time wasted or their distress increased by attending something that we might reasonably predict would be of no help.

As we have already seen, it is difficult to honestly predict whether counselling will definitely help in a particular circumstance. Nevertheless, there are times when counselling is clearly not the first or only appropriate INTERVENTION. It is doubly difficult to appear to turn someone away when they arrive because sometimes:

- part of their distress might be that they have difficulty feeling understood and valued
- they may lack self-confidence and a rejection would damage it even more
- they have been to other types of helper and they think that counselling is their last hope
- they are so desperate they might consider suicide.

However difficult it might be, we have to be completely honest with clients if we think counselling is not going to help. It would be wrong to let them find out after a number of sessions, after which they might feel that they are to blame for not trying hard enough. The use of counselling should be questioned if it is likely that their symptoms of distress are caused by external factors such as:

- poor housing or homelessness
- poverty
- lack of opportunity due to discrimination or oppression.

Problems of this nature are best addressed by social action. The counsellor as a citizen shares responsibility with all other members of society to remove these blocks to people's physical and psychological wellbeing.

It would be convenient if we could divide problems up into two neat categories: those of psychological origin (and amenable to counselling) and those of non-psychological origin (and therefore not amenable to counselling). However, there are some other causes of distress that, although they will not be solved by counselling, will undoubtedly be helped by counselling in that the person concerned will be able to function better with the kind of support that counselling can provide. It may also be that the client experiences repetitive patterns of self-defeating thoughts and behaviour that render them less effective in dealing with problems that do not have a psychological origin. It might also be that a person would be better able to challenge an oppressive system if they felt personally empowered, and counselling can sometimes achieve this. Such problems include those caused by:

- poor health (a physical illness or ORGANIC CONDITION)
- oppression and discrimination, including bullying
- living in an abusive relationship.

Counsellors must be constantly vigilant to ensure that their work with a particular client or clients in general is not contributing to disadvantage, abuse and oppression by rendering people more acceptant of poor conditions, whether at work or at home.

Psychologists must join with persons who reject racism, sexism, colonialism and exploitation and must find ways to redistribute social power and to increase social justice. PRIMARY PREVENTION RESEARCH inevitably will make clear the relationship between social pathology and PSYCHOPATHOLOGY and then will work to change social and political structures in the interests of social justice. It is as simple and as difficult as that (Albee, 1996, p.1131, cited in Davies & Burdett, 2004, p.279)!

What is 'personal growth'?

Counselling in the UK has become associated with what might be called the 'personal growth industry'. Self-improvement has been a feature of our society for 100 years or more and includes such initiatives as the Workers' Educational Association supporting the educational needs of working men and women. More recently, further education has embraced more non-vocational courses and reflects the fact that, as we get more affluent, we have to attend less to the business of mere survival. We can turn our attention to getting more out of life and, along with other self-development activities, improving our psychological wellbeing proves to be a popular choice. Furthermore, when people have a good experience as a client, they sometimes see that learning to be a counsellor could be a further step in self-improvement.

This 'personal growth' use of counselling contrasts with counselling as a treatment for more acute forms of psychological distress, as listed on pages 2–3 above. It is, however, no less worthy or ultimately useful. Fulfilled, happy citizens, relating positively to themselves and others, able to put good helping skills back into their communities, are an asset, not a handicap.

'Counselling' and 'psychotherapy'

Within the therapy world, there are numerous debates about whether 'counselling' and 'psychotherapy' are the same thing and, if not, what the differences are. For the purposes of this text, we will treat these two activities as synonymous. However, because many practitioners within the pluralistic field refer to their practice as 'therapy' rather than 'counselling', we will use the word 'therapy' throughout the remainder of this text.

Using the glossary

You will have noticed that some words are set in SMALL CAPITALS. This indicates that the glossary on page 110 carries a brief definition and explanation of the term. The SMALL CAPITALS can appear anywhere in the texts, quotes, subtitles or index.

Client work

To ensure anonymity, details of clients have been changed and disguised throughout this book.

Chapter 1
What is pluralistic therapy?

Pluralistic psychotherapy (or counselling) is, as its name implies, based on PLURALISM – a philosophical approach built on the belief that 'any substantial question admits of a variety of plausible but mutually conflicting responses' (Rescher, 1993, p.79).

A pluralistic approach to counselling and psychotherapy challenges belief in 'truths' about what will work in therapy, with its view that there is unlikely to be one single approach to therapy that is better than another for all clients. If one approach cannot be best for all clients, then there is a responsibility for therapists to find a way of working that ensures that they provide the best therapy for each individual client.

Pluralistic therapy is a framework for INTEGRATION in counselling and psychotherapy practice undertaken to optimise flexibility in therapy and benefit to clients while being grounded in a clear ethical stance and set of principles. It is a relatively new approach that allows the therapist to draw on a wide range of theories and theoretical understandings of clients' problems and practical ways of working so the therapy fits the client. The centrality of client involvement in this process is fundamental to the approach.

These ideas are consistent with the central guiding principle in pluralistic therapy itself: that the therapist works with whatever the client brings and their interventions are guided by the client's choice of GOALS, direction and purpose. It is the responsibility of the therapist to draw on the panoply of therapeutic approaches and resources available to them to find ways of working that provide the best therapy for each individual client. Moreover, what the individual client may need may change over time – that is, what is helpful for a client at one time may not continue to be so. Pluralism also supports the idea that no client can or should be required to confirm with some generalised notion of 'clienthood' to fit the assumptions and beliefs of the therapist.

The pluralistic approach is rooted in HUMANISM (McLellan, 1995; Cooper & McLeod, 2011a). Humanists believe that all people have the capacity for self-awareness and self-knowledge and the ability to use their intellect and free will to act for the betterment of themselves and others (Marx, 1977). The pluralistic approach also aligns with the 20th century philosophies that reject positivist and modernist ideas. For example, POSTMODERNISM argues that all truths are either *relative* and dependent on individual viewpoints or *pluralistic* – namely, there are many available truths that are equally valid and true. POSTMODERNISM also asserts there is no such thing as objective, absolute truth, as all knowledge is rooted in and influenced by the specific historical contexts and cultural discourses in which it is situated. Similarly, METAMODERNISM (Vermeulan & van den Akker, 2010) argues for the PLURALISM of all truths and seeks to understand and contain even opposing ideas and conflicting positions with a hopeful attitude and openness towards possibilities for constructing new meaning and positive change (Vermeulan & van den Akker, 2010).

Pluralistic therapy emerged from the proliferation of counselling and psychotherapeutic schools of thought and approaches over the course of the 20th century (Dattilio & Norcross, 2006; Prochaska & Norcross, 2018). There are an estimated 500 different therapeutic modalities in existence today. This multiplicity is supported by professional narratives that emphasise difference rather than similarity, with a resulting neglect of appreciation of the most effective and, often, common features of the therapeutic work (Lazarus & Lazarus, 2019; Norcross & Alexander, 2019). This 'SCHOOLISM' is seen as potentially undermining to therapeutic work because it narrows the scope of practice and the ways in which a therapist responds to the client.

According to the research evidence, all therapies are in fact roughly equal in their clinical effectiveness. This has been called the 'dodo bird effect' (Luborsky et al., 1975). No one approach to therapy is consistently more effective than all others for all clients and problems (Fernandez-Alvarez et al., 2016). Some may be more effective than others for specific issues, but overall clients tend to benefit more from therapies that fit their understanding of their problem and meet their preferences for how it is delivered (Cooper, 2008).

Development of pluralistic therapy

The application of PLURALISM to counselling and psychotherapy began in the late 20th century, but it was only in 2007 that Mick Cooper and John McLeod published a review and proposal for PLURALISM in counselling, and not until 2011 that they produced an introductory book on the framework and its origins, with guidance for practice (Cooper & McLeod, 2011a).

The complexity of a framework that allows for a wide range of therapeutic activities was addressed in the first handbook (Cooper et al., 2016) – a highly applied text providing further discussion on the relationship between PLURALISM and a range of therapeutic models, and how to work using the approach in various contexts and with different client groups. In parallel to this, there has been a recognition that many practitioners are already working pluralistically, without necessarily identifying with the approach – so pluralistic therapy can be seen as an articulation of what is already the case (see, for example, Stoll & McLeod, 2019).

These texts provide a framework for how pluralistic therapy can work in practice. In their 2011 book, Cooper and McLeod emphasised their wish to avoid the creation of another school of therapy. So, you can be a pluralist without practising pluralistic therapy – that is, you can have a pluralistic philosophy or stance without applying Cooper and McLeod's framework (Thompson et al., 2017). Having a PLURALISTIC STANCE means the practitioner agrees that there are many valid ways of working in therapy and that different ways fit different clients at different times, but may continue to practise according to their core model (although they may be open to referring a client on to a different practitioner or source of support). A therapist might also work pluralistically using a singular approach if they are able to adapt to a client's preferences and incorporate principles such as flexibility and COLLABORATION within their existing model.

Pluralistic therapy formalises a phenomenon that research tells us is already mostly the case: that, across the board, practitioners do tend to respond to what clients need rather than what their training and theoretical approach dictate. While professional narratives and literature often follow 'SCHOOLIST' lines, around 85% of practitioners in counselling and psychotherapy use techniques and interventions from different schools of therapy to meet their client needs (Zarbo et al., 2016). Indeed, the research evidence is so strong that some see the INTEGRATION of a range of METHODS and approaches as the only ethical stance for therapeutic practitioners (Finnerty et al., 2018; Wakefield et al., 2020).

In order to bring the client perspective into the therapy, a COLLABORATIVE approach is required, along with a rebalancing to equalise the role of therapist and client knowledge within the relationship. Within a single session the pluralistic therapist will adapt and adjust their practice according to information provided by the client and the shared understanding of what is going on. Across sessions, the therapist will be working on providing the activities and outcomes judged by the client to be helpful and will tailor their relational responses and activities to the client preferences and GOALS. So pluralistic therapy is not simply about deciding what a client needs and undertaking activities accordingly; it is about continually enabling the client involvement in therapy and responding to clients' preferences and feedback about what is helping.

Pluralism and integration

There is a clear distinction between pluralistic therapy and INTEGRATIVE approaches. Integrative models draw on evidence from research and practice to create new approaches to therapy (Norcross & Goldfried, 2019). So, for example, COMMON FACTORS *models* are built on the research evidence for an identifiable number of factors common to all therapy approaches that account for their effectiveness and can be seen as the active ingredients of therapy (Laska et al., 2014; McLeod, 2018). Technical ECLECTICISM (Lazarus & Beutler, 1993; Lazarus et al., 1992) applies techniques taken from different approaches, based on what has been shown to help others with similar presentations, without concerning itself about the psychological theories on which the techniques are based. *Theoretical* INTEGRATION involves a merging of the theories and techniques of two or more psychotherapies into a whole new therapy approach (Prochaska & DiClemente, 1982; Stiles et al., 1990; Wachtel, 2014), with a new or amended explanation of why it works. *Assimilative* INTEGRATION involves integrating techniques and principles from other orientations into an existing approach, resulting in a new therapy with its own theoretical foundations and rationale. For example, Safran and colleagues (Safran & Muran, 2006) developed CBT to create a more relational form of COGNITIVE THERAPY.

By contrast, pluralistic therapy provides a framework that permits practitioners to draw ethically on different aspects of the multiplicity of therapy approaches and interventions to create an individualised, flexible programme of therapy that is aligned to clients' needs and preferences. It does not seek to articulate a new theory of problem development and resolution and change or create a 'new therapy' to deliver it. Rather, it integrates by drawing directly on aspects of therapy that are shown empirically to make a difference to the individual client. It privileges the ethical stance of prioritising the *individual* needs and preferences of the client and structures the deployment of the therapist's skillset accordingly. Central to this process is that how pluralistic therapy is undertaken and what is done are decided with the client, rather than by the therapist, as is the case with most INTEGRATIVE models.

Because PLURALISM has an open and deliberately self-questioning stance towards truth and encourages dialogue with different ideas and practices in therapy, the nature of the pluralistic approach and the understanding of how it is applied in practice is constantly evolving. As a result, understanding pluralistic therapy is more about developing an appreciation of the flexibility and values of the approach.

Chapter 2
Key principles

The pluralistic approach integrates multiple forms of knowledge and practice. Rather than having a fixed set of rules for practice, it is guided by a set of principles. These key principles act as reference points for practitioners.

These principles originate from an ethical perspective, value base and research findings on how clients experience therapy and what they report as being helpful. The pluralistic approach does not assert exclusive ownership of these principles, but they are useful to help the practitioner and student conceptualise the approach.

1. An ethic of care

An ethic of care is a foundational principle of pluralistic therapy, rooting the approach in a deep and genuine caring for others and a responsiveness to the client's preference and needs:

> ... we need to start questioning by asking how we can do good to the Other... the question of how we act towards each other in caring ways is the most important question, and should be where thinking starts. (Cooper, 2020).

Pluralistic therapy embeds a principle of care and ethical awareness into the actual practice of therapy, drawing on a relational ethic that foregrounds the client's individual context and their cultural values and beliefs, perspectives and feelings (Gabriel & Casemore, 2009; McLeod, 2018).

A pluralistic ethic of care can also be understood as a commitment to creating a positive therapeutic relationship characterised by good communication, co-operation, compassion, understanding and 'give and take'. This is 'care' as a primary value, not simply a tool to make the therapy more effective.

Along with a genuine desire to engage with clients in helpful, respectful and empowering ways, pluralistic therapy also seeks to engage pluralistically across the profession. This chimes with its opposition to SCHOOLISM. The pluralistic stance views difference and even conflicting ideas as bringing value and learning, and seeks to work respectfully and collaboratively with colleagues across the field.

2. The primacy of the client

Rooted in this second principle is the recognition of the primacy of the client's perspective, needs and active involvement in the therapeutic process. Clients are seen not as passive recipients of therapy but as co-therapists who bring significant knowledge and resources as active participants working to achieve therapeutic change (Cooper & McLeod, 2011a).

This principle also incorporates respect for individuality and recognition of diversity in cultures, contexts, experience and response. The therapist undertakes to act in ways that are informed, respectful, COLLABORATIVE and helpful to the client. These commitments are prioritised over the therapist's beliefs and opinions and are linked to a fundamental commitment to developing a breadth of knowledge and understanding, while also acknowledging, where appropriate, any lack of understanding.

The primacy of the client is also recognised in the understanding that, simply by their seeking help or assistance in their lives, they are 'heroic' (Duncan et al., 2004).

3. Recognition of diversity

The principle of the primacy of the client in turn means that pluralistic therapy both honours and facilitates respect for difference and diversity and is committed to equality in the therapeutic relationship. This principle requires that therapy is a conduit for inclusivity and accepts all truths and experiences as equally valid. It also means that therapists understand and acknowledge the impact of the broader societal context on the client and the therapeutic encounter and reflect on the role of therapy in the political landscape. For example, socio-cultural differences will influence the therapeutic relationship in terms of power and perceptions of 'otherness' and the silencing of some experiences, ideas and possibilities.

4. Multiplicity of approaches – the best way of doing therapy is the one best suited for the client

Pluralistic therapy believes that there is no one globally effective or superior model of therapy. There are many models and theories of psychological distress, therapy and change processes and they are equally valid and can co-exist without the need to compete with or detract from each other or become one single, 'best' model. Thus, the pluralistic approach is able to draw from all bona fide therapeutic approaches, and can, indeed, include any method or activity that has meaning for the client and therapist (Cooper & McLeod, 2011a). It can do this because it is a perspective on therapy as a whole, rather than a specific way of doing therapy (Cooper & McLeod, 2011a). Thus, therapists from a range of integrative and non-integrative modalities can work pluralistically if they work in ways that are underpinned by pluralistic values and principles.

Because PLURALISTIC PRACTICE has developed to view all theoretical approaches as potential 'truths', pluralistic therapists can draw on ideas and understandings from many different approaches if they may be helpful to build a client's understanding of their situation. Therefore the pluralistic therapist needs to have the capacity to deconstruct and assimilate ideas and practices that are outside of their current assumptions (McLeod, 2018) in order to apply them helpfully with clients.

This principle also holds that there is no single, right way of conceptualising clients' problems. Different understandings can be useful for clients at different points in time, but the most helpful way to begin to make sense of a client's difficulties is to start with their perspective and understanding of what they think the problem is and what has caused it.

PLURALISTIC PRACTICE draws on explanations and understandings of distress from many different fields – from relational, developmental, spiritual, physiological, cultural, socio-economic and social justice perspectives. Therapist empathy and cultural humility are key to understanding difficulties from a client's perspective, and therapy can enable new understandings and insights to develop that draw on both client and therapist knowledge.

5. Uniqueness of experience – different people need different things at different points in time

Clients are unique individuals subject to unique socio-cultural contexts and have different needs, preferences, values and perspectives that will develop and change over time through learning and experience. The pluralistic approach holds that this uniqueness should be acknowledged, embraced, encouraged and celebrated (Cooper & Dryden, 2016).

A pluralistic therapist assumes that different clients may need different approaches at different times. For example, one client might benefit from a structured approach at the start of therapy, whereas another might need a more process-orientated approach. An approach that worked previously might not always be effective for the same client. This principle requires a focus on dialogue and feedback to identify what a client prefers and needs.

6. Knowledge – multiple types and sources of knowledge can be helpful

This principle values multiple forms and sources of knowledge. These include *common knowledge* – knowledge that is published and generally available about various ways of helping; *client personal knowledge* – includes insight, experiences, resources and client preferences, and *therapist personal knowledge* – all that a therapist has learned and developed through training, practice and life experience. There is a deep, principled and ethical commitment to valuing the client's own knowledge, resources and experience as well as the knowledge, expertise and ideas that a therapist can draw on and offer to the client.

The pluralistic approach shares the humanistic stance of 'not-knowing' (Schmid, 2001). This is not about lack of knowledge; rather, it is an appreciation of multiple forms of knowledge that allows the holding of one perspective while learning another or the ability 'to tolerate the co-existence of knowing and not-knowing' (Cooper & McLeod, 2011a, p.141).

Rather than prioritising either therapist knowledge or client knowledge, the most fruitful position acknowledges client and therapist knowledges as of equal primacy. This shifts therapy away from a predictive and imposed model of change towards a genuinely exploratory and authentically COLLABORATIVE endeavour. It is a process of helping a client locate and articulate knowledge and knowing how to contribute therapist knowledge without overshadowing the client's strengths and resources (McLeod & McLeod, 2016).

7. Individualisation – therapy is likely to be more helpful when it is individualised

This principle describes the need for therapist responsiveness and flexibility in order to create a therapy that fits the client. Identifying what a client wants and doesn't want in terms of both the process and outcome of therapy and adapting one's approach to client needs and preferences is seen as an ethical responsibility in PLURALISTIC PRACTICE. This can even include accommodating a client preference for less COLLABORATION.

Therapist responsiveness and adaptation is crucial not only to make therapy more effective but also to avoid harm (Norcross & Wampold, 2018). Pursuing GOALS in therapy that clients do not share, using METHODS or techniques that clients don't agree with, and exerting control over the direction of therapy without their agreement all have the potential to harm clients (Curran et al., 2019).

Individualising and adapting in response to client preferences means that PLURALISTIC PRACTICE cannot be homogenised but will, by definition, be idiosyncratic and unique to each client. A therapist may respond differently to client A than to client B as clients and therapists co-create individual relationships in response to each other. Pluralistic therapy and the therapeutic relationship are by nature collaboratively designed and specific to each client and therapist.

8. Relationship – therapy is likely to be more effective when the relationship between client and therapist is characterised by trust, collaboration, care, and respect

This principle relates to the consistent finding that therapy tends to work best when there is a strong relationship between client and therapist to support it (Norcross, & Lambert, 2019). Pluralistic therapy highlights the significance of the relationship while recognising that clients may need different ways of relating. For example, some clients may need less empathy, and others may need more empathic attunement (Cooper & McLeod, 2011a).

The therapeutic relationship in pluralistic therapy is based on COLLABORATION, which is central to ethical practice (Gabriel, 2016). Central to COLLABORATION is engagement, equality (as far as is possible) and dialogical process. Engaging a client's active involvement in collaborating and co-creating a new understanding or strategy can stimulate change in and of itself (McLeod, 2018). The COLLABORATION can represent a mutuality of experience, with the sharing of knowledge, distress and exploration. Clients can then become more able to recognise their own preferences and make active choices around the direction and nature of the activities, and can therefore shape the therapy in ways that are more helpful for them.

9. Therapist reflexivity

Pluralistic therapists need a high degree of self-knowledge

around their own beliefs and assumptions about therapeutic change, to avoid misreading or neglecting their clients' perspectives (Cooper & Dryden, 2016). They need to be self-aware and capable of self-monitoring in the immediate term and reflective in the longer term around how they think, feel and act within the therapy and towards the client. For the client to be empowered to be an active agent in therapy, the therapist needs to be able to sustain the COLLABORATION, support the client to become an active agent, respond to their preferences and SHARE DECISION-MAKING, while being part of the evolving therapy. They need to be able to stay within an emotional relationship while also using their experience with the client to understand and inform the therapy. To do this requires reflexivity.

The flexibility required by pluralistic therapy can place an additional load on the therapist, and an ability to monitor resilience and self-care is essential.

10. Flexibility – in therapeutic structure, process, communication and relationship

By its very nature, as a human process, therapy involves unpredictability and uncertainty. Like all other approaches, pluralistic therapy is characterised by messy connections and disconnections, moments of depth and ruptures.

In pluralistic therapy, clients are encouraged to explore and state their individual preferences, which stimulates creativity, a flexible response and the development of insight. Trust is key to being able to hold an adaptable, relational process that invites and contains the uncertainty, risk-taking, learning, messiness and unpredictability from which a genuine synergetic co-creation can emerge.

Chapter 3
Problems in living

People come to therapy usually because aspects of their lives are causing them distress and they wish to make changes in how they feel, think and behave and in their circumstances and how they relate to their experience. The pluralistic approach conceptualises psychological problems, emotional distress, the absence of wellbeing and mental health diagnoses as 'PROBLEMS IN LIVING'. This phrase aims to do away with implications of deficit and broaden the understanding of what can be problematic to a person. The pluralistic approach recognises that explanations for distress may be spiritual, cultural, societal, environmental, relational, cognitive, emotional, experiential, and physiological, and that interventions can be targeted at any of these levels. This can seem overwhelming to the novice therapist but, in practice, the explanation that is best aligned to the client's understanding is likely to be the one that has most meaning and significance for them, and so this is a good place to start.

The pluralistic therapist applies the following assumptions:

- Counselling and psychotherapy theories are just theories – they have no objective truth, but ideas can be drawn from them to aid the therapist's understanding of the client's experiences.

- Clients construct their problem stories from their understandings, experience and the context of therapy; therapists and clients draw on theories to deepen and enhance meaning.
- Therapy allows the creation of new stories, new understanding and new meanings.
- How the client understands their problem and the meaning they give to it can help create ideas for how it may be resolved.
- The therapist needs to be able to understand how to apply theory to understand the client experience, but the focus should remain on ideas that are helpful to the client.

Particular aspects of PROBLEMS IN LIVING are also relevant to a pluralistic understanding:

- PROBLEMS IN LIVING manifest in many different ways, depending on the client's circumstances and how they interact with their experience.
- Client problems will usually have developed over some time, sometimes imperceptibly, until they become intolerable. The problem is likely to be a very familiar part of the person's life.
- A client often turns to therapy when the ways they usually resolve the problem cease to work.
- The person will have existing strengths and an understanding of how they have managed the problem up until now, and may also have ideas about what will help – this can be a good place to start.

In pluralistic therapy, it is helpful to think about how to address PROBLEMS IN LIVING in simple terms that are rooted in the client's experience.

~ What's the problem?

~ Why is it there?
~ What do we think we can we do about it?

Then, once ideas have been shared about what might be done, the client and therapist can ask:

~ Shall we try that?

Reaching a shared understanding of the problem is often the most important part of therapy. When a client begins therapy, they usually start by describing their experience and the problems they are facing. From a pluralistic perspective, the therapist has at their disposal a vast range of theoretical explanations for those PROBLEMS IN LIVING. All schools of therapy provide explanations for the development, emergence and perpetuation of problems, but how useful they are to the client will depend entirely on how relevant and meaningful the client considers them to be.

Mental health and diagnosis

For some clients, their PROBLEMS IN LIVING are most usefully described in terms of a diagnosis, such as depression, anxiety or PTSD, for example. The notion of diagnosis is contentious and contended (Johnstone, 2000; Johnstone & Kopua, 2019), especially in counselling and psychotherapy, because it assigns objective categories of psychiatric 'illness' to groups of people whose actual experiences will be very subjective and may be hugely varied. So, a doctor might regard psychological problems and diagnoses through a theoretical cause-and-effect framework – for example: 'You have low mood, poor sleep and are having suicidal thoughts, therefore you are depressed and will benefit from a course of antidepressants/CBT.' A pluralistic therapist will start with the client's life circumstances: 'You are unhappy, sleeping badly and having suicidal thoughts. What has happened to you and how has this contributed to your emotional state?'

Pluralistic therapy seeks to get underneath the diagnosis to understand the client's life in the same way that the client does. Pluralistic therapists are not just interested in how a client experiences their problems but also in how the client explains them. Clients in therapy may present their PROBLEMS IN LIVING as a story of things that they believe are not going well or should not be happening; they may also have associated aims for how they would like to feel or how they would like things to be going – this is all essential information for the pluralistic therapist. Additionally, while the client's experiences and explanations are key, aspects of client presentation or behaviour in the room and relational behaviours can provide important insight into the person, the nature of their problem and how it is impacting on them.

The heroic client

The pluralistic approach aims to ensure that clients engage and draw on their own strengths and resources during therapy, and that the therapist will work to help this happen (Sparks & Duncan, 2016). In pluralistic therapy, the client and therapist work with the notion of the 'HEROIC CLIENT' (Duncan et al., 2004). This sees the client as an actively striving, choice-making, COLLABORATIVE co-therapist who is able to aid the process of therapy and without whom there would be no progress (Bohart & Tallman, 1999).

Bohart and Tallman's research on outcomes from therapy (1999) led them to conclude that effective therapy derives from the client directing and setting their own GOALS and having a sense of choice and empowerment. This is in total conflict with the diagnostic approach, which assumes a deficit in people experiencing difficulties: that they need to be helped by others or that there is a biological or psychological fault in their functioning and behaviour that must be discovered and corrected. Pluralistic therapy seeks to recognise and celebrate the client's strengths and positive attributes, opening up opportunities for them to be an active agent in their own therapy and encouraging them to question and challenge the therapy and to feel that their perspectives and responses to what is going on are not just valid but an essential aspect of getting it right. All therapies strive to empower the client variously with insight, knowledge, options and change, but pluralistic therapists explicitly and overtly recognise the client as self-healing, proactive and resourceful and therefore the subject of therapy, not the object.

Cultural embeddedness and client experience

Complementary to the concept of the HEROIC CLIENT is the overt recognition in pluralistic therapy of the client's cultural capital – their networks of support, personal and other resources, opportunities and potentiality. Because it is designed to incorporate a broad range of understandings of problematic events and experiences, and because it is an ethical stance based on equality and inclusivity, the pluralistic approach necessarily emphasises action against social exclusion and inequalities (Winter et al., 2016).

Pluralistic therapists acknowledge the socio-economic and cultural context of the client, not simply in terms of class, demographic, gender and race, but with a more fine-tuned sensitivity to aspects of the client that constitute their life-world. The reasons for this are three-fold: it helps them understand the structure of the problem and the possibilities for solutions; it provides rich opportunities for understanding and exploring experience that may be relevant, and it helps the client and therapist locate and draw on cultural resources that may also be currently or potentially helpful.

Chapter 4
The collaborative relationship

The therapeutic relationship is seen variously as both the conduit through which therapy is experienced and also as an essential ingredient of change in therapy (de la Prida, 2020). Pluralistic therapy uses the COLLABORATIVE RELATIONSHIP as the foundation for practice. Essentially, it is what creates the therapeutic alliance (Berger, 2017; Horvath, et al., 2011; Norcross, 2011) with the HEROIC CLIENT (Duncan et al., 2004).

There is rich evidence for the effectiveness of the therapeutic alliance across schools of therapy (see, for example, Flückiger et al., 2012; Horvath, et al., 2011; Muran & Barber, 2010; Norcross, 2011). A pluralistic therapist prioritises what are agreed in the literature to be the key components of the alliance (Bordin, 1979; Flückiger et al., 2012) (see Chapter 5):

- agreement on GOALS
- agreement on TASKS
- establishing and maintaining a positive therapeutic relationship.

The collaborative process

In order to understand the COLLABORATIVE RELATIONSHIP as an evolving interaction, it is helpful to draw on the notion of the *co-therapist* (Duncan et al., 2010). A client who acts as a co-therapist is able to use their own expertise to interpret, plan and undertake action alongside the counsellor. This stance optimises the benefits of the therapeutic alliance by enhancing the opportunities to locate what might help and reduce limitations on what can be achieved and how (clients are unlikely to exclude methods from other theoretical schools or to encourage the use of methods that are not directly meaningful and helpful to them). Therapist responsiveness and ability to adapt are crucial, not only to make therapy more effective but also to avoid harm (Norcross & Wampold, 2018).

There is a range of actions pluralistic therapists can use to enhance the COLLABORATIVE aspects of the therapeutic relationship and manage ownership of their expertise. To support the client's influence, agency and role in the therapy process, therapists can explore the client's ongoing or earlier solution strategies (e.g. 'What was helpful in managing this previously?'); underline the client's choice and authority (e.g. 'It is important that this is the direction you find most helpful'), and explicitly share decision-making (e.g. 'What shall we do here?'). They can demonstrate collaboration by changing how they express themselves and using tentative phraseology or 'hedging' (Oddli & Rønnestad, 2012), rather than directive or conclusive statements. They can also throw light into the 'black box' of therapy by describing their methods to their clients before using them, to set the scene for what is going to happen, and 'walk' the client through them.

In such ways, the pluralistic therapist will carefully navigate their role as 'expert' in the COLLABORATIVE RELATIONSHIP. Therapist knowledge and skill remain key components of the approach, but it is how the knowledge is used that is important. Both client and therapist bring experience and knowledge when they develop an understanding of the problems the client brings and undertake therapeutic work. Underlying this is the therapist's ability to describe the rationale for activities and the changes that different methods may achieve and how. In addition, when collaborating on therapy activities, the therapist may use their own knowledge and experience to challenge the client on their self-perceptions or ways of managing problems, but these challenges will not be corrective; rather, they will comprise methods like reframing and taking active steps to present to the client an alternative way of thinking (Oddli & Rønnestad, 2012). In many ways, the pluralistic approach highlights that neither the therapist nor client 'know more' but that both 'know different'.

Box 4.1 offers a case study to illustrate the different kinds of knowledge within the pluralistic therapy relationship referred to in Chapter 2:

- *common knowledge* – knowledge that is published and generally available about various ways of helping
- *client personal knowledge* – knowledge that includes insight, experiences, resources and client preferences
- *therapist personal knowledge* – all the knowledge that a therapist has learned and developed through training, practice and life experience.

Case study 4.1: Use of knowledge

> Debi experienced a traumatic sexual assault as a child. At the age of 23, she sought therapy with Ash because of her increasing low mood and relational difficulties. She and Ash drew on knowledge from a range of sources.
>
> ***Client knowledge***: Debi brought her experience of the events and her understanding of the context of what had happened in terms of her own family. This was drawn out through the therapeutic conversation. She also brought her knowledge and ideas of how her experiences impacted on her. She knew too how a friend of hers, who had similar experiences, had coped by taking them to therapy.
>
> ***Therapist knowledge***: Ash had knowledge of ways of working with survivors of sexual assault. She used her experience of

working with other clients who were survivors, in terms of processing her emotional responses and establishing a sense of control and safety; her knowledge of the 'zone of tolerance', and ideas around attachment, which helped her understand how the therapeutic relationship might be impacted. During the therapy and between sessions, she worked with her supervisor to improve her understanding of what might be happening for Debi.

Common knowledge: Debi had already found some informative websites for survivors of sexual assault and brought to therapy the ideas she had drawn from these. Ash helped her decide what was useful for her to make sense of her experience and the options open to her around reporting the historic events. Together they found some books written by survivors that helped validate Debi's experience.

The COLLABORATIVE RELATIONSHIP has its foundations in the ability of the therapist and client to share a space that is creative, safe and tailored to the client. The structure provided by the therapist and the tapping into all forms of available knowledge is part of a more complex picture where the pluralistic therapist adapts their therapy to fit the client. McLeod (2018) proposed Brown's (2009) stages of design as a helpful way to understand this process in PLURALISTIC PRACTICE:

1. Creating a therapeutic space for 'mistakes'

This allows recognition both for things not working and being able to talk about them, while also setting the scene for 'trying things out'. It relies on META-COMMUNICATION and the use of multiple channels for feedback and is supported by an attitude of reassurance, support and cultivating expectations and hope (Cooper & McLeod, 2011a; Norcross & Lambert, 2019). Therapists can model to a client that it is okay to get things wrong and be congruent in expressing being unsure and confused, making mistakes and even creating ruptures. Seeing the therapist as being able to get things wrong without self-judgement can be an important experience for a client.

When a client starts to try out new things, both in therapy and in their life, it suggests a change in self-perception and confidence. A pluralistic therapist can adopt a solution-focused or change-focused approach and help the client plan and enact changes. However, therapy also provides a space for an exploratory and sometimes parallel process, where clients can try out new things and new ways of relating within the therapy. Examples might include the therapist helping the client run through a conversation in role-play or giving a congruent response to a client trying out different ways of being or communicating, like expressing anger, or allowing themselves to ask for their own needs to be met.

2. Observing and learning from the client

This concerns both engaging and learning about the client, and also learning with the client. As with all therapies cultivating curiosity and a genuine interest in the client, their life and their difficulties are an important quality for a pluralistic therapist. It involves paying attention to what the client says and actively seeking to identify their knowledge and resources, but also initiating exploration into aspects of experience that neither of you understand. Additionally, being open to learning from the client is crucial to collaboration. The therapist is told by the client what their experience is, what their preferences are, and how they choose to progress. Each time this occurs, the therapist learns something about the nature of the client's problems, how to shape therapy in helpful ways, and where the potentials lie for how a client might change and improve their life. This is an incredibly valuable part of being a therapist, in part because what is learnt from clients can vastly enrich and develop practice. Experiential and practical knowledge, personal development and unique methods can be developed in this way.

3. Generating ideas and possibilities

The pluralistic approach is inherently co-creative and this process flourishes when a diversity of perspectives is valued. Blunden (2020) emphasises this sense that the therapeutic space supports a process that can be over-simplified as COLLABORATION or SHARED DECISION-MAKING when it is, in fact, a messy practice of negotiation, ongoing communication and sharing of ideas and experiences. This relies on the creation of a space where the client is able to feel comfortable and safe, and can be an exciting aspect of therapy as the therapist responds creatively to the client and vice versa, so innovative solutions emerge.

Collaboration and creativity in pluralistic therapy is not simply about what happens in the room; other features of the therapy are open for negotiation. Does the client want weekly, seated, 50-minute sessions in a room involving dialogue and relational intimacy, or are there other ways of working that they would prefer or benefit from? Sometimes clients will come with a clear idea of how things would work best for them, drawing on prior experience or knowledge of preferences, but equally clients may need to know what options are available and how open the therapist is to providing them. The approach is therefore open to variance and accommodation for the client, suggesting ideas based on knowledge but not imposing assumptions according to client presentation (see, for example, Box 4.2).

Case study 4.2: Openness to client preference

> Faisal has been working with Maxine, a single mother of two young children. They have been working online as Maxine finds it easier to have sessions at home when the children are asleep. Faisal notices that Maxine is often tired and sometimes disengages before the end of a session. Maxine mentions that she feels more positive after sessions, but that it only lasts a few days, and that 'a week seems like a very long time when you are depressed'. Faisal responds creatively by asking if Maxine would prefer to have two sessions a week. Maxine thinks this is a great solution but cannot afford to pay more and so they negotiate having two 25-minute sessions instead of one 50-minute session. Maxine really appreciates that Faisal has flexed his usual orthodox practice; it helps her feel that she matters, and the shorter sessions fit better with her life. They

> find this solution works well as Maxine is able to engage more fully in both sessions.

Relational pluralism

It is clear that the nature of the relationship in pluralistic therapy is fundamentally COLLABORATIVE. However, the interactions between therapist and client also impact on the process of change and application of methods. All therapy schools promote client-therapist relationships with somewhat different characteristics and these underly how the therapy functions (Beutler & Consoli, 1993). So, if a pluralist therapist is to apply strategies and methods with clients, they need to incorporate an understanding of this relational dimension. A useful concept for this RELATIONAL PLURALISM is the relational chameleon (Lazarus, 1993): the pluralistic therapist allows the changing needs of the client to guide the way they behave and responds without losing the sense of openness and congruence.

An example of this is the case of Paula who embarked on pluralistic therapy with the GOALS of accepting that she had diabetes and that she should undertake the life changes and medical interventions needed to manage her disease (Smith et al., in press). The therapist adopted a series of relationship positions over the course of the therapy, depending on the client TASK and METHOD at the time. In practice, the shifts between the relational positions were difficult to distinguish but they were characterised by different use of language, expression, pace and intonation, as might be seen in the difference between therapists applying different modalities of therapeutic interventions:

- Counsellor as comrade – the therapist draws on her own experience of having diabetes to validate and contrast with those of the client. The client reports feeling understood.
- Counsellor as mentor – the counsellor provides information to the client about her understanding of the medical impact

on non-adherence to diabetes medication. The client states that this is a very helpful 'wake-up call'.

- Counsellor as collaborator – the counsellor gives the client 'homework' to support behaviour change and action planning for doing things differently.
- Counsellor as crucible – the counsellor provides space and safety for the client to explore the aspects of her experience and emotional processes. The counsellor patiently holds the parts of the client's self that are in conflict as she works through the issue.

The range of relational stances in Paula's case, while not depicting an expected or necessary repertoire, illustrates the purpose of adaptation. In pluralistic therapy, the characteristics of the relationship will depend on the methods used at the time. For example, if the client requires a safe, open reflective space to explore their experience, the therapist is likely to adopt a holding, accepting and empathic stance. If the client is needing help in structuring their plans for behaviour change, the therapist will need to be more guiding, prompting and future-oriented. If the client wishes to undertake a more interpretive stance, seeking not just to explore but to theorise on how to understand their experience, then the therapist and client will share ideas and put their 'heads together' to explore them. In some cases, the relationship can be recognised as the method of change, but it also can become the subject of a developing understanding: for example, through the observation of transference and countertransference. Any functional impact or observations of relationship changes can be spoken about:

> 'So if we go ahead with the idea of me challenging you to keep on track, like when you go off topic, I am going to sound a bit bossier than I usually do. Can we check in on how that feels?'

That said, while the PLURALISTIC FRAME is COLLABORATIVE and the stance of the therapist is dependent on the needs of the client and the TASKS and METHODS in hand, the relational style of the pluralistic therapist will fundamentally depend on their personality and training, the needs and presentation of the individual client and their relational style.

The function of the relationship between therapist and client and the portfolio of relational styles is in theory limitless. But no therapist would adopt a stance that feels unintuitive and incongruent; the therapist will remain alert to the relationally driven changes and adaptations that are happening in the moment. An aspect of this is the process of adjustment between relational stances to suit the methods and activities being undertaken. A pluralistic therapist will balance the needs to be themselves, to adapt to the client and to adopt stances that facilitate the process. It may be a useful separation for the therapist to articulate in supervision – 'This is who I am with this client' – and also observe when changes are needed or undertaken – for example, the need to be more or less directive, which can occur during the walk through or introduction to the METHODS. For example, the therapist might say:

> 'When we are talking about the loss of your mother, I am going to try and make sure I keep a reflective space. I will just be allowing you to get in touch with your emotions, keeping quiet, and we can see what emerges.'

Or:

> 'If we look to work with this idea that you speak from two different positions with an aim of moving your decision forward, I will be asking you some questions and directing the activity a bit.'

Along with the monitoring of relational dynamics, pluralistic therapy expects the therapist to recognise divergence and address ruptures in the therapeutic relationship. While concordance is not always the goal, the process of creating a shared understanding must come from two perspectives, and ruptures occur when there is a negative impact of unexpected misalignments on small and large scales. Ruptures in therapy are not uncommon and they do have a significant impact. In one study, participants who were dissatisfied with their therapy (38% of the total number of clients) reported 'ruptures not being addressed' in around 60% of cases (Nilsson et al., 2007). Another study found that taking responsibility to address ruptures involves validation of client experience and exploration of the situation, and that the adoption of changes to interpersonal interactions and reflection on behaviour and response patterns were felt to be useful for future strategies (Eubanks et al., 2018). Because of the collaborative stance, it is common practice for a pluralistic therapist to recognise ruptures and pause and explore them in the moment, but also adapt to the learning obtained by the experience:

> 'Can we pause a sec? I think what I said there about you feeling guilty about not seeing your mum didn't help. I wonder if it landed badly for you?'

Shared language, meaning and metaphor

Pluralistic therapy requires a sensitivity and skill in the use of language. This is for several reasons. The first is that, in order to collaborate, the impact of language must be recognised, managed and monitored. There is a responsibility for the therapist to adapt how they communicate to the client's manner of expression, in the first instance to avoid a perceived power imbalance. A client who is presented with explanations that are not clear for them will be hindered in their knowledge, but also may perceive a difference in language use as a barrier. For example, it may flag up educational or social differences that may be unhelpful, particularly in the early stages of therapy. Second, collaboration and shared understanding requires a shared language to reference experiences through the use of metaphor. Shared phraseology serves to underscore the collaboration and also enhance the potential for creative responding. And, finally, pluralistic therapy requires a sensitivity to the constructive elements of language. From a constructionist or constructivist perspective, communication is not an objective representation of other things but is integral to the process of creating what is (Friedman, 1993). The creation of positive self-referencing stories and articulation and rehearsal of preferred narratives is an important outcome of therapy, as evidenced in the work of narrative therapists who aim to support the client in constructing and deploying alternative and more helpful stories about themselves (Freedman & Combs, 1996; White & Epston, 1990). Pluralistic therapists co-create and co-construct narratives with their clients and similarly provide the space for new, positive stories to be told.

> 'I know now I am not the useless, stupid, crying person they told me I was, but the independent, smart, emotionally intelligent person I talked about in therapy.'

The primary means of communication in therapy is talking but clients may have different needs in terms of communication. The adoption of expressive pluralism (Schmid, 2001) aligns to the need for flexibility and adaptation. Communication can be adapted to individual clients' needs and preferences, alongside other aspects of the therapy. For example, some clients might find it helpful to have a mix of email, text and talking; others may benefit from creative non-verbal methods of expression, depending on the task and method at hand and personal preferences. An openness to communication between sessions can also be helpful, particularly when a client wishes to provide feedback; some clients find it helpful to express feelings when they occur between sessions, which they can text or email, and these can be explored at the next session. These preferences may also accommodate the need for distance in a client who finds difficult feelings or experiences easier to articulate indirectly and would benefit from the disinhibition effect of working online (Suler, 2005).

Meta-communication and shared decision-making

As will be explained in the next chapter, client preferences are explicitly sought in relation to the structure of the therapy process, the relational and interactional processes, and the methods used. This relies on the META-COMMUNICATION and elicitation of feedback in a variety of forms. The principle of collaboration influences the attitude of the pluralistic therapist towards the client throughout and is based on the valuing of client strength and client voice and explicit acknowledgement of how the client is striving towards their GOALS within their own life context.

The practice of META-COMMUNICATION is not unique to pluralistic therapy; it occurs in a wide range of contexts. However, it is the primary conduit through which COLLABORATIVE working is established and maintained in practice (Cooper et al., 2016) and how SHARED DECISION-MAKING occurs. Meta-communication is the practice of talking about what we are doing, so is a method of both framing and pausing the 'action' of the therapy conversation to observe, reflect on or navigate through what is occurring. Meta-communication occurs around different aspects of the therapy at different times and for different reasons. However, overall the practice ensures that the therapist's and client's perspectives are communicated, that the therapist responds to client preferences, and that there is a shared understanding of the purpose of therapy.

Meta-communication is distinct from SHARED DECISION-MAKING, in that the latter refers to how choices are made through using the knowledge and perspectives of both therapist and client in order to accommodate client preferences and GOALS. Shared decision-making is reliant on META-COMMUNICATION within a COLLABORATIVE RELATIONSHIP.

Common points of META-COMMUNICATION during pluralistic therapy include the start of each session, when a discussion will take place about what the client would like to focus on and the therapist checks in on any activities occurring between sessions. During any one session, the therapist or client may comment on the process – for example, pause to allow SHARED DECISION-MAKING to undertake a particular direction, to state a perspective, or to observe what they feel is occurring. The therapist or client may comment on their own experience or ask the other to share a felt sense or reaction to something that has occurred or been expressed. At the end of the session, a pluralistic therapist and client are likely to discuss how they felt the session went, and (in the way that suits the client) talk about how the session may have helped or hindered the therapeutic process to aid the therapist in creating the best way of working for the client.

META-COMMUNICATION can also take place between sessions, using other media and platforms. For example, some clients may wish to provide updates or feedback via email or text, having had time to think about what has happened in the therapy session, or to report something that has developed between sessions.

Shared decision-making

In pluralistic therapy, the relationship between therapist and client is not only COLLABORATIVE but must also involve SHARED DECISION-MAKING about matters to do with the process and progress of therapy. This aspect of therapy is nurtured from the very start and can be tricky to balance in a relationship where the knowledge of what the choices are is almost always with the therapist. Examples of decisions include the focus of the activity (e.g. what the client wants to talk about or work on); what the client wants to achieve (GOALS and TASKS), and how the client wishes to work on them (METHODS); whether and how to amend the relational aspects of the therapy (e.g. does the therapy need to be more action focused and, if so, how can the therapist facilitate that?), and the practical aspects of the work (e.g. should sessions be weekly, should contact be made between sessions, when should the therapy end?).

In an important study of clients working with pluralistic therapists (Gibson et al., 2020), researchers explored this process of SHARED DECISION-MAKING. Clients reported that they consciously experienced decisions as shared and that their therapists supported them in being active in the decision-making process. To do this, the therapists shared the position of possessing relevant and 'expert' knowledge, and clients felt recognised and able to engage in the decision-making process. However, it was also noted that the notion of being engaged in the decision-making process needed to be developed over the course of therapy and that clients needed support to grow into this position. This indicates that the hard work of COLLABORATIVE RELATIONSHIPS involves an early commitment to enhancing the client's ability to make choices and be involved in discussions when the way forward is being decided.

Chapter 5
The process of pluralistic therapy

As previously emphasised, pluralistic therapy is, essentially, a framework for the INTEGRATION of a range of approaches tailored to the individual client's needs and preferences. This framework comprises a number of key elements: FORMULATION, GOALS, TASKS and METHODS, and feedback. These are used to create a shared understanding of the client's difficulties, motivations and aims, an evolving and collaborative plan of action for the therapy and a means for continuous monitoring of the client's preferences and experience of the therapy. This chapter will look in more detail at these elements of the therapy process.

Pluralistic therapy has been accused of being simply a selection of activities drawn from a range of schools delivered by practitioners who are 'Jacks of all trades', who use and discard METHODS and ways of working without a coherent thread to the therapeutic process (this is discussed further in Chapter 8). As this chapter will demonstrate, this is far from the case: there is a central coherence to the pluralistic approach, but it is not one based around a model of a particular school of therapy; rather, the consistency lies in the application of its principles.

Beginnings, middles and ends

The more the client knows about therapy before it starts, the better. Research demonstrates that clients who have a good understanding of what to expect in therapy are likely to engage for longer and to greater effect (Barrett et al., 2008), and that what happens during the pre-therapy phase is likely to have an impact on the client's engagement and outcomes (Swift & Greenberg, 2015). So, from the start, there is an emphasis in pluralistic therapy on information-sharing in order to prepare the client. This is likely to include:

- information about what the therapist or service offers and what this will look like for the client
- an explanation of the purpose of counselling and what changes it might bring about for the client (instilling hope)
- an explanation of how the client's preferences may be accommodated in the first instance (instilling empowerment and the concept of choice)
- reflective exercises to encourage the client to think about how they might like to work.

Pluralistic therapy also uses a number of techniques to establish the collaborative nature of the work and empower the client from the very start. These are likely to include:

- the development of a collaborative FORMULATION, often including a TIMELINE, and shared understanding of the client's PROBLEMS IN LIVING and GOALS
- an exploration of previous experiences of therapy, what has helped them in the past and under what circumstances
- a discussion about what might be helpful to do in therapy and/or about the issues the client is facing
- an exploration of the client's strengths and resources, which may be returned to as the therapy progresses
- some explanation and an overview by the therapist as to the practicalities of how they work
- an explanation of feedback mechanisms, ensuring that the

client understands the purpose of this and how and when they prefer this to be done.

Defining characteristics of the therapy serve to reinforce the shared understanding and collaboration that is central to the pluralistic approach:

- Formulation anchors the process for therapist and client in a shared and fluid understanding of what is going on that is updated and revised as needed to reflect the process of the work.
- Sessions are structured around META-COMMUNICATION and agreed activities, linked to TASKS that are identified through the FORMULATION, and how these TASKS are undertaken is collaboratively agreed.
- The process of therapy is monitored and reviewed, and the purpose and results of the TASKS and any changes of emphasis and direction are discussed collaboratively with the client.
- Successes and progress are acknowledged and celebrated.
- Use of EXTRA-THERAPY RESOURCES is explored and clients are encouraged to seek out and follow up opportunities for these.
- The COLLABORATIVE RELATIONSHIP is continually monitored for breaks, ruptures and opportunities for learning.

Case formulation

CASE FORMULATION is a formal psychological term for what is simply the gathering together of the client's experience and the creation of a plan (however informal) of what therapy might do to help. Different theoretical perspectives have different traditions and understandings of what CASE FORMULATION comprises, but no therapy progresses without an understanding of what the client's difficulties may be and what kinds of activities will be undertaken to address them. CASE FORMULATION in some form has been found to be important to ensure the client's needs are met and reduce the risk of drop-out (Eells, 2007; Nilsson, 2007).

CASE FORMULATION in pluralistic therapy follows the principle of individual uniqueness and the ongoing evolution of a shared conceptualisation of the client's PROBLEMS IN LIVING, how they came about, and what the client would like and find helpful. It also forms the platform for deciding TASKS and METHODS (McLeod & McLeod, 2016).

There are three steps to effective CASE FORMULATION in pluralistic therapy:

1. the description of the client's story and experiences
2. the sharing of interpretations, reasons and explanations of the key elements of the story in relation to the PROBLEMS IN LIVING
3. the collaborative making of decisions about the focus of the therapy and how it is delivered, linked to the agreed GOALS, TASKS and METHODS.

The FORMULATION in pluralistic therapy is co-owned and provides an externalised, transtheoretical representation of the client case. It is a representation of client experience but is likely to have some elements of theoretical interpretation and cause-and-effect links drawn from a range of theoretical perspectives ideas and knowledge. So, for example, an explanation for a client's anxiety might be framed within their early life experience (drawing on attachment theory) and the perceptive biases they may have developed (drawing on CBT). A client with a poor sense of self-worth in a relationship might understand this as being a result of having conditions of worth imposed on them (drawing on person-centred therapy) and can work on these by examining their own ego-states when interacting with others (drawing on transactional analysis).

Externalising the FORMULATION in a written, drawn, listed or mapped depiction of the client's case is important to the collaboration between therapist and client as it allocates shared ownership. Representing it in some way that is mutually accessible is preferred by many pluralistic therapists and clients. One way of doing this is the TIMELINE FORMULATION. This, while not an essential component of pluralistic therapy, is a helpful tool for many practitioners and clients.

Timeline formulation

Usually, a TIMELINE FORMULATION can be initiated at the point at which the client has told the therapist enough about their life for the therapist to distinguish the relevant information and sketch this (commonly, two or three sessions into the work). It establishes the information at hand and allows initial direction for therapy to be tentatively agreed. It sets the scene for the therapist to talk about their understanding of what is going on for the client during the early sessions and allows the client to see what is going on for them and flag up to the therapist if they are failing to see something, appear inconsistent, or are heading in the wrong direction. Clients often report the creation of the TIMELINE as a significant moment in their therapeutic journey as it constitutes a first step in understanding and validating much of their experience.

Collaboration on the TIMELINE is seen as essential so the therapist can garner the reactions of the client and any feedback and amend and adapt it accordingly. Some clients choose to 'take the pen' and construct or reconstruct the TIMELINE in a way that makes more sense to them and their experience. Others are happy to use the therapist's record of the FORMULATION to guide the progress of the work.

During the early stages of sketching a CASE FORMULATION, a therapist may begin to explain some hypotheses that have emerged from the client story to create links between the aspects of information on the TIMELINE. In conversation, aspects of life history will lead to ideas about intrapersonal and intrapsychic patterns, but the therapist will also have some sensitivity to 'markers' of particular problem types, such as relational issues, affective/experiential misalignment and reactions/behavioural challenges (Kennedy-Moore & Watson, 2001). These hypotheses may be drawn from theoretical knowledge, from observations and also from the cause-and-effect relationships indicated by the client's explanation of what is going on. It is also important to note the aspects of the story that seem to be important but are not yet explained, or suggest missing pieces in the puzzle. These primary hypotheses should be presented to the client for thought and discussed in terms of their validity from the client perspective.

This process also allows for the clients to express their desires for particular TASKS or aspects of their experience to be addressed and their preferences for the direction and ways of working.

Goals, tasks and methods

The GOALS, TASKS and METHODS structure is used in PLURALISTIC PRACTICE to make sense of the therapy. Each goal can be reached by a range of TASKS, and each task is undertaken using a range of METHODS, depending on the skillset or 'MENU' of the therapist and the preferences of the client.

Using the metaphor of a journey, the client GOAL is where they are heading, the TASKS are the roads and routes that might be taken and the METHODS are the vehicles used to make the journey – so, car, bus, train or walking. Each destination can be reached via different routes (the long and winding, scenic one, or the fast, direct one), and the routes can be navigated at different speeds (Ford Anglia, Lamborghini, bicycle). Each journey will depend on where the client wants to go, how they want to get there, and the capacity of the therapist and client to work with particular METHODS (or vehicles).

It is important to explain in detail what it meant by these terms within the PLURALISTIC FRAMEWORK as they are often misunderstood as prescriptive and overly structured aspects of the therapy process. In fact, they are simply a way of understanding the purpose and process of therapy.

Goals

The purpose of pluralistic therapy from the perspective of the client is their personal and agentic striving towards their collaboratively determined GOALS. Goals are the desired outcomes of therapy, being as they are future-oriented and related directly to personalisation of therapy and the client capacity for choice around what they want to achieve (Cooper & Law, 2018; Klein et al., 1986; Lambert & Harmon, 2018; Mackrill, 2010).

Therapy GOALS tend to fall into one of five categories (Grosse Holtforth & Grawe, 2002; Hanley et al., 2016):

1. coping with specific problems and symptoms – e.g. 'I want to feel less depressed'

2. interpersonal and relational issues – e.g. 'I want my relationship with my partner to be better'

3. wellbeing and functioning – e.g. 'I want to feel more comfortable with my body'

4. existential issues – e.g. 'I want to explore why I don't believe in God'

5. personal growth – e.g. 'I want to improve my self-confidence'.

Some important things to note about GOALS:

1. Therapy GOALS relate to the client's reason for coming to therapy and their desired destination; they are highly individual, embedded in client experience and form the foundation of the TASKS undertaken.

2. Research has indicated that clients who reach agreement with their therapists on the GOALS and TASKS of therapy early on do better than clients who do not (Greenberg & Watson, 1998). However the client preference for working with GOALS is also influential, suggesting that this too is important (di Malta et al., 2019).

3. Generally, a positively articulated goal is more helpful than a negatively articulated one: for example, 'to reach a point where life feels manageable day to day' is probably better than 'to stop being so chaotic', because this defines the destination.

4. Goals are outcomes of change processes and can occur on different scales and under different time frames, but tend to fit with the client's underlying values and hopes (Cooper, 2019)
5. Goals may represent important aspects of political or socio-cultural experience, so prioritisation of cultural background and an understanding more broadly of what this might mean for a person can be essential. So, for example, some cultures will prioritise individual outcomes over societal ones.
6. Life GOALS tend to be linked to underlying assumptions and values around how life should be lived. A desired life-goal might be to live well, to be of benefit to society or the world, or to minimise one's footprint on the earth. These GOALS inform and have value for the therapy in that they provide a sense of priority for the client. All choices are made within the context of the overarching 'reasons of living'.
7. GOALS change over time and over the course of therapy, as the client develops their understanding of their experience and perhaps better understands what might be achievable in therapy. Pluralistic therapists use FORMULATION as a live understanding and the evolution of GOALS for the client is viewed as a natural feature of the process.
8. GOALS help move clients from hopes and intentions towards change actions and help structure activities into manageable TASKS and monitored progress (di Malta et al., 2019).
9. Having a sense of direction and purpose is in itself fulfilling – having just a sense of going somewhere is often in itself therapeutic (Cooper, 2019).

The use of GOALS in pluralistic therapy has been challenged, and you could question whether clients can consciously and consistently know what it is they want from therapy (let alone life). A pluralistic therapist will be neither dogmatic about the requirement to articulate GOALS nor dismissive of the client's capacity for self-knowledge, but will remain aware that therapy has a purpose and that understanding that purpose is important. Research indicates that GOALS work best when the client is comfortable and motivated to work with them, when their expectations of possible outcomes are well managed, and when there is flexibility in the goal-orientation of the therapy (di Malta et al., 2019).

Tasks and the task taxonomy

TASKS represent the things that need to happen or be undertaken to reach the GOALS. In the absence in pluralistic therapy of a predetermined theoretical model of how to attain a particular client outcome, TASKS provide a link between what the client seeks and how the activities in therapy get them there. They emerge from the collaborative FORMULATION shared between the client and therapist.

Both client GOALS and TASKS can be conceptualised within a spectrum running from personal and immediate changes (shift in current emotional state) through longer-term changes in ways of being (developing understandings or behaviours that reduce or improve experience of difficulties), to life-long, spiritual and profound holistic changes (deep shifts in ways of perceiving and responding to the world).

As can be seen in the example of Janet (Box 5.1), there are direct links between the client GOAL, the TASKS being proposed and the range of METHODS that can be used. Collaboration ensures that there is a conversation about each of these TASKS, what the activity entails and what the purpose of it is, allowing the client to make informed choices about what might be helpful and also paving the way for process monitoring. Ultimately, there is fluidity around the process, which relies on the therapist having the ability to articulate the choices on offer and develop with the client an understanding of how they fit and what they might do.

Case study 5.1: Janet's goals, tasks and methods

> Janet came to therapy for help with her addiction to drugs. She described her abusive childhood, troubled teenage years, and current seven-year relationship to her partner, who was also struggling with addiction. Her goal was to become 'clean' and get a paid job. Her therapist discussed with her what she might need to do to get 'clean' and then get a job.
>
> **Task 1**: Generate the ability and resilience to undertake methadone treatment.
>
> **Task 2**: Improve Janet's emotional regulation in order to reduce the frequency and seriousness of the times when she felt driven to use drugs.
>
> **Task 3**: Work on Janet's self-esteem to enable her to 'go out in public' and 'be a normal person'.
>
> The discussion then turned to METHODS: how these three TASKS might be addressed, how they were interlinked and which should come first. Janet was keen for tasks 1 and 2 to be first, and felt that they were closely related to one another. She felt that achieving them might help her start on task 3, but that this last task might be looked at further down the line as she could not face doing them all together. METHODS suggested by the therapist for achieving the TASKS included:
>
> ### Task 1
>
> Method 1: **gathering information** from the NHS and her social worker to understanding how she might get on a methadone programme.
>
> Method 2: **talk with the therapist to improve her understanding** of the barriers and challenges she experienced in her previous attempts at coming off drugs and how she might overcome them this time.
>
> Method 3: **Talk through current experiences** to become more aware of her tolerance and resilience, what makes

her feel strong, and what helps her feel able to make her own choices.

Task 2

Method 1: use **in-the-moment monitoring of emotional processes** linked to physical sensations to become more aware of emotional states and the desire to ward off some thoughts and experiences.

Method 2: raise tolerance of unwanted emotional experiences by using resources such as **relaxation and yoga**.

Method 3: **keep a diary of triggers** to examine patterns of substance use and unhelpful behaviours, with a view to devising strategies for change.

Method 4: **talk through painful childhood experiences with the therapist** in order to build Janet's tolerance of her memories of what happened, create distance from and understanding of those experiences, and lessen their power to drive her to use drugs.

Task 3

Method 1: **create a mood board** to record aspects of self that might be seen as positive (on her own or with help of the therapist).

Method 2: **talk through** the possibility that negative self-identity is an unwanted judgement and that Janet can refuse it and become more aligned to a more positive sense of self.

Method 3: **brainstorm and plan** opportunities to experience positive events between sessions, record them in a diary and bring them to the therapy.

An important development within the pluralistic approach has been the creation of TASK LISTS to aid the client's understanding of the therapy process. The taxonomy of TASKS proposed by Cooper and McLeod (2011a) provide an abstracted list of the kinds of activities clients generally find helpful in therapy. Table 5.1 illustrates how this can be used to demonstrate the links between TASKS and METHODS, drawing on a range of different therapeutic models and approaches. In practice, the therapist can suggest METHODS that they are confident in using and best suit the client's needs and preferences for ways of working.

Table 5.1: Task taxonomy with example methods

Making meaning: working through an issue in order to understand things better
- Therapist use of COUNSELLING SKILLS in listening and reflecting back meaning and emotion (person-centred therapy).
- Projective techniques (psychodynamic therapy).

Making sense of a specific problematic experience
- Talking through the event and sharing interpretations and ideas (generic COUNSELLING SKILLS).
- Describing the event and working to attach emotional experiences to the sequence of events (emotion-focused therapy).
- Exploring metaphoric expressions for the events and people within the experience to better understand and accept what happened (narrative therapy).
- Linking patterns within the event to the actions of the current time (psychodynamic therapy).
- Exploring difficult experiences and emotions non-verbally (creative arts).

Problem-solving, planning and decision-making
- Articulating the issues, and examining the possible causes and solutions on offer (solution-focused therapy).
- Writing pros and cons or other representations of the decision (motivational interviewing).
- Exploring and researching information that would be helpful in making plans or decisions (cognitive-behaviour therapy).

Changing behaviour
- Talking through current behaviour patterns and proposing alternatives (cognitive-behaviour therapy).
- Working with the therapist to plan and carry out behaviour experiments or alternative actions (cognitive-behaviour therapy).

Negotiating a life transition or developmental crisis
- Using space to explore the process and what it means emotionally; allow for grieving (person-centred therapy).
- Exploring alternative identity formulations that would enable the transition to be more positive (person-centred therapy).
- Honouring moving on from one state to another (Gestalt therapy).
- Using existential theory and/or spiritual beliefs to broaden the frame and create new meaning to life-journey (Cooper, 2020).
- Exploring the tensions left over from a disrupted passage through a life stage and examining how these needs can be functionally met (psychodynamic therapy).

Dealing with difficult feelings and emotions
- Using the core conditions to allow space and time for emotional exploration (person-centred therapy).
- Using emotional focusing techniques to locate felt-sense emotions and recognising/articulating these in order to incorporate them into experience and allow impact to recede (person-centred therapy).
- Exploring alternative METHODS of expression of emotions to allow processing (creative arts).

Finding, analysing and acting on information
- Working with therapist to decide what is needed and how it might be found (generic COUNSELLING SKILLS).
- Talking through and evaluating information, linking it to relevance in client's own life and using this to move forward in functional ways (cognitive behaviour therapy).

Undoing self-criticism and enhancing self-care

- With the therapist, mapping out the client's perceptions and labelling of self, challenging negative ideas and picking up on unhelpful negative self-talk and criticism (cognitive-behaviour therapy).
- Examining the developmental experiences that contributed to the client's negative sense of self in order to understand the learning processes that created it, thereby empowering the client to move beyond it (person-centred/psychodynamic therapies).

Dealing with difficult or painful relationships

- Talking through relationship patterns to allow an interpretation and possible adjustment (transactional analysis).
- Examining patterns of transference and assumptions around others in relation to self, and interpreting where these patterns came from and how they might be changed (psychodynamic therapy).

Table 5.2 lists the TASKS suggested for James, a client with early-stage dementia, to help him achieve his overarching goal of accepting and coming to terms with his diagnosis.

Table 5.2: Tasks suggested for James

Area of work linked to goal	Tasks/activities
Retaining a sense of 'self'	Finding out who I am and who I am for others
	Finding out what my diagnosis means to me
	Exploring whether I can be me with dementia

Facing my death	Express my emotions
	Grieve for what I have lost
	Address specific emotional difficulties as time goes on
Coping with symptoms	Look at barriers to 'living normally'
	Explore and establish ways of managing or coping with cognitive and behavioural changes
Dealing with health care and broader social attitudes	Make sense of my medical care
	Make choices about what will occur going forward (power of attorney)
	Understand the dementia narrative in society (and think about rewriting it)

Methods and how to understand them

METHODS in pluralistic therapy are essentially the activities used to address the TASKS and so bring about change. They can be defined simply as 'ways of doing something'. Some serve to strengthen the relationship and aid therapeutic engagement; some are designed to improve the clients' ability to engage with their experience and deepen insight; others are designed to address specific difficulties or help a client do things differently. In pluralistic therapy, METHODS are not linked to a particular theoretical model; rather, they are used because they are considered by the therapist and client to be most likely to help with the task at hand. This provides a liberal palate from which to choose.

Cooper (2016) lists the basic METHODS used in pluralistic therapy as follows:

- establishing GOALS
- active listening
- expressing acceptance and care

- minimal encouragers
- reflecting, paraphrasing and summarising
- asking questions
- using symbols and metaphors
- working in the here and now
- helping make sense of experiences
- helping people re-evaluate what they do
- helping people re-decide.

Research into everyday therapy practice indicates that therapists tend not to stay rigidly within the confines of their modality in their choice of METHODS (Thoma & Cecero, 2009). Pluralistic therapy allows a therapist to be creative with their METHODS and ways of responding to client needs and employ the 'trial and error' approach described in Chapter 4. In Box 5.2, an experienced pluralistic therapist describes some of the METHODS she uses in practice, and the purpose and rationale for using them. It illustrates the flexibility of the pluralistic therapist in adjusting their METHODS in response to client feedback and being creative in what can be done in addition to the 'core' COUNSELLING SKILLS (McLeod & McLeod, 2011). No two pluralistic therapists will give the same answer to the question 'What methods do you use?'

Case study 5.2: 'What methods do you use?'

> I rely on a range of METHODS and tend to use them where it feels like it would be useful and meaningful for the client and within my competence. Beyond the standard COUNSELLING SKILLS, I routinely use therapeutic letters where a) the client struggles to remember what the session has been about; b) as a way of 'reframing', and c) to support clients to move from a fixed position to a more open one. At reviews, clients often talk about using them as sources of support during times of distress. From my perspective, they are about validating experiences and supporting clients to consider strengths.

I've written a play with a client as a METHOD of supporting a person who loved theatre and needed the space that projection allows. The task was to understand the contradictory aspects of herself. She said it helped her shift to a more accepting place. This client initially thought two-chair work might help her access that sense of integration, but in the moment it was too much – hence the play.

I use immediacy and my own felt sense with clients where their goal is about getting in touch with their authentic self. I would only use it in certain cases for certain reasons, and only where there is a sufficiently robust relationship with a client, of course. I might say something about 'noticing being pushed away when I get close to X, Y or Z' and encouraging the client to notice in the moment what they are experiencing in their body. Where a client seems to be struggling to articulate, I would encourage them to create something with postcards, art material, stones etc. I've invited clients to draw their dreams when that has seemed helpful. With anxious clients, I have invited them to make sensory boxes in session where thought record sheets, for example, haven't been especially useful. I'm into 'walk and talk' where a client is struggling to be in the room and/or they get a sense of being grounded when moving.

I use the relationship a lot – how we are experiencing each other in the moment based on what's being said, gender and so forth. This way of working has seemed useful for clients whose goal is to relate differently.

There are also some less conventional 'METHODS' that clients have talked about being useful. I have taken my make-up off with a client – that felt 'right' at the time and seemed to be 'the most helpful bit' for the client. She wanted to grow her self-acceptance and felt unacceptable unless she was fully 'made up'. We kind of did a 'let's explore this together' thing to see how it felt to be less made up together. It felt risky but we were taking the risk together.

> With permission, I carefully reflect body language with clients as a way of accessing any unconscious material. I remember all the fancy METHODS I used with this one particular client, but what she remembered was the time I modelled her hand gesture and asked what she was letting go of. She got in touch with an early memory of being told she was too big to hold her dad's hand and she physically remembers her hand being rejected. It seemed that she was able to make the link between that moment and the visceral felt-sense of her current difficulty asking for help.

Therapy menu

A crucial part of pluralistic therapy is being able to identify whether what the therapist can offer matches what a client wants or needs, where there are gaps in skills or knowledge, and what other resources and knowledge may be needed. Cooper and McLeod use the concept of a MENU (2011a), which communicates the idea of therapy offering a range of options that could meet a client's preferences and needs. The MENU doesn't contain a pick-and-mix selection of hundreds of therapies, and it doesn't mean a pluralistic therapist has to do everything a client wants, but it does invite dialogue about what a client might want. The MENU essentially shows what the therapist can offer, prompts dialogue around client preferences and guides what the therapist does with the client.

Pluralistic therapy does not distinguish between activities that are 'therapy' from those that are 'not therapy' on the grounds that anything that is helpful to the client can be considered therapeutic, and in some cases it may be more therapeutic than the therapy itself (Cooper & McLeod, 2011a). Originally termed 'cultural resources', but often now described as 'EXTRA-THERAPY RESOURCES', a multitude of options can be seen as therapeutic by a client, and these usually reflect the client's socio-cultural and lived experience. The process of discovering or rediscovering resources with the client, understanding why they are helpful in the context of the client's life and how they can be used in the therapy and after is an essential aspect of pluralistic therapy.

Examples include religious practices, such as attending church, prayer and pilgrimage; physical activities, such as swimming, yoga, sports and sex; creative activities, such as painting, writing, music or cookery; personal care, such as shopping for clothes, applying make-up or having beauty treatments; reconnecting with nature, such as gardening, walking or beachcombing, and identity and relational activities, such as keeping a diary, blogging, connecting with social groups and writing letters.

In practice, these EXTRA-THERAPY RESOURCES are likely to carry personal meaning for the client and will in many cases serve to become an aspect of their ongoing self-care. This identification and engagement process is more than simply the recognition or recommendation of things that might help; alongside, there needs to be an accompanying discussion of whether this activity fits the client, what it might achieve, and what the meaning of this would be to the client. The therapist is likely to be checking in with the client on the activities as the therapy progresses and linking them to aspects of the 'in-the-room' METHODS. This focus on EXTRA-THERAPY RESOURCES is something that fits the HEROIC CLIENT approach; the sharing of stories and ideas about cultural resources, what people have done, and still do to support themselves in creative and unique ways illustrates the heroism that occurs every day.

Feedback

As frequently mentioned throughout this book, checking in and checking back with the client is a constant process in pluralistic therapy, to ensure that the GOALS, TASKS and METHODS remain relevant and helpful to them. Seeking client feedback has been shown to improve therapist-client alignment and outcomes in all therapy (Lambert & Harmon, 2018; Lambert et al., 2001). A common method of undertaking this is the use of feedback reports and questionnaires that clients can complete before and after sessions to flag up what they find helpful, track progress towards their GOALS and highlight the need for any changes in terms of topic and priority.

The invitation to feed back to the therapist is characteristic of pluralistic therapy. Research on client deference has pointed to a common misalignment of therapist and client understandings about the therapy and preferences for how it is carried out (Rennie, 1994). This underlines the importance of establishing feedback systems throughout the work, especially as clients may find direct, face-to-face feedback challenging. There is a wide range of different ways of inviting and encouraging feedback, including sessional feedback forms where the client can rate how helpful the session was, how much progress they feel they have made and their preferences for working. One such form is the Cooper-Norcross Inventory of Preferences (C-NIP) (Cooper & Norcross, 2016), which can be found in Appendix 2 at the end of this book.

While clients welcome having a range of ways to feed back their experience of therapy, there is a risk that the use of client preference forms may mean therapists feel they have to unquestioningly respond to what the client wants and that they become unduly self-critical (Bowen & Cooper, 2012). This issue is much debated within the pluralistic approach. It is wrong to think that the pluralistic therapist is expected to do only what a client wishes in all circumstances. Rather, the preferences conversation is seen as providing an opportunity for the therapist to gain insight into how the client understands their needs, how they would like to proceed and how this can be done in collaboration with the therapist. Simply accommodating a client's preferences without discussion is not the aim or purpose of seeking feedback; its aim is to establish a space for a conversation about how to make the therapy better for the client.

Chapter 6
The process of change

Pluralistic therapy is no different from other approaches in providing the space and time to explore and engage in new ways of being. However, because this approach explicitly allows the therapist and client to draw on a wide range of understandings of what is going on and how the client might be helped, it reframes the concept of therapeutic change. A pluralistic perspective on the processes of change asks:

- What can be done to help the client know, see, or perceive things that will help them understand their problems and situation?
- What can be done to help the client change or accept their emotional or perceptual experience?
- What can be done to help the client think of themself in positive and meaningful ways?

Pluralism adopts a generic approach to what changes in therapy, so GOALS can be met in several ways, but there are commonalities to what happens. Usually, clients will want to develop insight and self-knowledge (with accompanying empowerment): for example, to make sense of situations and relationships, see themselves differently, recognise patterns, and tap into out-of-awareness or subconscious knowledge and experiences. Clients may undertake emotional processing and articulate felt-sense experiences, or locate difficult emotions and express and come to terms with them. They may also wish to explore new ways of acting, dealing with or thinking about issues or themselves or make new connections between aspects of their lives (Castonguay & Hill, 2007; Hill et al., 2012).

Ultimately, clients can leave therapy with a new understanding of themselves, of others and of their situation and experiences, having changed their expression and responses to experience or behaving differently because of learning or changes to awareness. They are likely to be deploying and using skills and information to sustain or change situations, as well as telling new stories to themselves and others that are more functional and beneficial (Levitt et al., 2016; Swift & Parkin, 2017). Clients will feel different after therapy, mainly in positive ways. There are many things that could happen during therapy that could constitute aspects of 'change' and, to some extent, pluralism 'black boxes' that might, in single schools of therapy, be clearly articulated change processes. However, it can be argued that this lends itself to a richer understanding of therapeutic change.

Rather than limiting potential change processes by adopting a single defined model, pluralism conceptualises change as a fluid, idiosyncratic process, occurring via many individualised pathways (Cooper & McLeod, 2011a). Some aspects of change will be predictable, but others will not. In pluralistic therapy, this results in a fundamental shift in focus away from routinised therapist activities towards a genuine dialogic exploration in order to collaboratively identify what might help facilitate change for each client, at that particular time. A defining characteristic of PLURALISTIC PRACTICE is that, by prioritising dialogue and the exploration of possibilities, the client and therapist can collaboratively map out multiple individualised 'change pathway'.

The uniqueness of each person's change process means that pathways for different clients with similar presenting issues will often be different. For instance, let's imagine that two clients come to therapy with the same goal of wanting to reduce stress and anxiety.

Case example 6.1: Aiden and Aaliyah's change pathways

> Aiden is single and a partner in a law firm. Aaliyah is living at home with her parents while training as a chef. Julia, the therapist, knows that talking about experiences in therapy can help clients to process feelings and develop insight (common knowledge and personal knowledge). She knows that yoga and running (EXTRA-THERAPY RESOURCES), can help with anxiety, because she has tried these herself (personal knowledge), and has read some studies showing that mindfulness can also help (common knowledge).
>
> Through CASE FORMULATION, Aiden identifies that talking and processing his feelings would be helpful (METHOD). He tells Julia that he already uses a mindfulness and meditation app (personal knowledge and EXTRA-THERAPY RESOURCES), but says he finds that, even after using the app, he is 'full of pent-up energy' and can't relax. Julia shares her experience of how running has helped her to manage anxiety (personal knowledge) and asks if it's something he'd like to try, and Aiden agrees. After several sessions, Aiden recognises a pattern of taking on extra work that contributes to his levels of stress and links it to his relationship with his father, who was 'hard to impress' (insight), recognising that impressing others is an underlying motivation that stems from childhood.
>
> In Aaliyah's CASE FORMULATION, she describes how she is 'constantly running all day' and feels physically exhausted but is unable to sleep because of 'over-thinking'. She doesn't think that talking about her feelings will help because it hasn't in her past experience of therapy, and she says she would like a more structured approach (preference). Julia shares her experience of yoga being helpful for alleviating stress (personal knowledge) and shares what she knows about mindfulness helping with anxiety (common knowledge). Aaliyah wants to try yoga but

wants to explore other strategies. They agree to use sessions to plan activities and explore other activities that she can try outside of therapy. During their exploration, Julia identifies that Aaliyah likes art (EXTRA-THERAPY RESOURCES), and suggests trying creative painting activities. Through these experiences, Aaliyah develops and shares an understanding of her own tendency to 'think too much' about things. Through the use of artistic METHODS, she finds alternative ways of representing her experiences instead of the thinking patterns that otherwise would have preoccupied her.

Aiden's unique CHANGE PATHWAY included running, which helped him to release some of his stress. The exploration of his past in therapy helped him develop insight, and consequently he became more able to decline taking on extra work at the law firm.

Aaliyah's unique CHANGE PATHWAY also included yoga, which helped her relax physically, while artwork was a helpful way to relax her mind. The structured collaborative approach helped Aaliyah feel that Julia really cared about her progress. This contributed to Aaliyah's motivation; she found the process empowering and this led to an increase in self-awareness and her ability to manage her own thoughts.

In order to explore what might be helpful to a client, it is important that both client and therapist are receptive, and that there is a transparent willingness in the therapist to engage in sharing ideas, knowledge and genuine responses to the client (Cooper & Dryden, 2016).

PLURALISTIC PRACTICE recognises that change can be an unpredictable process and can occur in unexpected or unplanned ways, stimulated by events outside of therapy or by actions and experiences within it. For example, a promotion at work or a new relationship can be powerful but unplanned stimulants of change. Ongoing recognition of the changes that occur, whether anticipated or not, can be incorporated into the collaborative assessment, FORMULATION and SHARED DECISION-MAKING. Indeed, these discussions can stimulate change in themselves by providing an opportunity for clients to reflect on their problems and resources and develop insight. It can also help by modelling ways of relating and being responded to that can be educative and therapeutic for clients (Cooper & Dryden, 2016). Ruptures and relational difficulties are a common unpredictable occurrence in therapy, and for some clients, resolving conflicts or misunderstandings can be an unplanned but significant reparative experience or developmental task (de la Prida, 2020).

Ultimately, all of the methods and theories used in therapy, or outside of therapy, to help alleviate distress derive from the richness, diversity, cultural heritage and history of human experience. Therefore, when thinking about what might help promote therapeutic change, pluralistic therapy specifically includes a wide range of strategies, ideas and resources – anything, indeed, that can be used as a METHOD to stimulate change.

Chapter 7
Training, professional development and supervision

Adopting a pluralistic approach does not require the removal, correction or overwriting of the knowledge and experiences of the qualified therapist. It asks only that the therapist is critically aware of their knowledge, skills and assumptions, and understands their impact on their ability to work with clients' own beliefs, understandings and life-world. So, for example, a pluralistic therapist who works primarily with a person-centred approach can draw on these skills, use these understandings and aid the client in person-centred ways, but can choose to have growth edges across any modality and learn to incorporate CBT methods to enrich their 'MENU' of choices for the client.

Over and above the core competencies expected from them, outlined in Table 7.1, most pluralistic therapists will have their own understandings of therapeutic change, but will recognise that theirs is just one perspective, or range of understandings, and the client may have another, equally valid perspective, and therapy is what happens between them. A therapist needs always to ask not just, 'What am I bringing to the party?' but also, 'What does my client bring?' Both have strengths that may be deployed in addressing the issues in hand. In many respects, this is an empowering message to a therapist, but it is also a signal that pluralistic therapy places a profound level of responsibility on the therapist to use their judgement wisely and maintain a high level of self-awareness. This means the pluralistic therapist is engaged in a continual process of learning, developing and evolving understandings and capacities to respond to client needs.

Table 7.1: Four competency domains essential to pluralistic practice

- Relationship skills – being able to develop and sustain an effective COLLABORATIVE RELATIONSHIP with a range of clients.

- Therapy process skills – being able to undertake activities relating to the stages of therapy, assessment, FORMULATION, client preference, process monitoring, maintaining boundaries, ethical decision-making, rupture repair and so forth.

- Conceptual abilities – being able to understand and articulate different ways of interpreting and understanding experiences for and with the client.

- Intervention skills and METHODS – being able to appropriately and effectively deploy a range of strategies, interventions and METHODS, and to amend and adjust these according to client feedback.

Working with difference

It is a responsibility of all therapists to be culturally sensitive and aware. However, the centrality of the principles of collaboration and shared understanding means that pluralistic therapists do not start from a position where the mainstream experience is assumed to be 'normal' and 'other' experiences are incorporated. Instead, they will acknowledge difference within the relationship, but also the impact of difference in context. A pluralistic therapist might say, 'I am different from you and you from me. Do we need to acknowledge that? What impact does it have on you and on us?' Pluralistic therapists work with a sense of their own socio-cultural identity and how this developed and is perceived by others, which then forms a point of reference for both difference and sameness, which can be treated with respectful enquiry. The client experience of the therapist within the equalities frame is at all times influential and a pluralistic therapist will ideally have the capacity to navigate conversations around these issues.

In order to enact this principle of inclusivity and client primacy, the concept of allyship is useful (Atcheson, 2018). Allyship occurs when a person holding privilege relating to their race, gender, education and abilities works in solidarity and partnership with a marginalised group of people to help take down the systems that deny that group's basic rights, equal access and ability to thrive in our society. For therapists, this relates to the conversations that should occur with perceived 'outgroups' who may be positioned as such as a result of their race, sexuality, gender, ability and perceived disability.

Allyship is linked to the pluralistic striving to see every individual as embedded in an unequal society (which may be to their benefit or detriment). It is not just about the pluralistic therapist's acknowledgment that particular groups face particular issues; it is the active engagement in practices that aim to establish equality and social justice within a particular field. A pluralistic therapist will not simply know that a client who identifies as trans-male will be subject to discrimination and negative judgements that may become internalised and impact on that person's wellbeing; they will have the capacity to lead on adopting the necessary semantics and language to ensure negative societal attitudes are not perpetuated in the therapy and, if appropriate, will speak out against prejudice and give active support by calling out injustice and advocating for the oppressed group.

Training in pluralistic approaches

It is possible to become a pluralistic therapist through a number of routes, depending on whether the practitioner is already trained in a single or integrative modality, whether they wish to train using a PLURALISTIC STANCE, or if they wish to train as a pluralistic therapist and use the PLURALISTIC FRAMEWORK for practice.

The development of a PLURALISTIC STANCE when training in a single modality is likely to involve:

- respect and valuing of the users of therapy and an appreciation of their involvement in the process
- a critical/affirmative perspective on counselling theories and modalities (Cooper & McLeod, 2011a), understanding one's own approach in relation to other approaches and being able to establish through dialogue what might be the best approach for any particular client.

Training in the PLURALISTIC FRAMEWORK is different. McLeod and colleagues (2016) suggest that any pluralistic training programme or conversion course should include:

- COUNSELLING SKILLS, including collaboration, negotiation and working with client preferences, and understanding when and how to use them
- reflexivity, self-awareness and relational capacity – the ability to provide a congruent, non-judgemental and empathic space and active engagement in use of feedback and the ability to form a COLLABORATIVE RELATIONSHIP with the client
- critical perspectives on theory and interventions – introduction to a range of perspectives on different counselling/psychotherapy approaches; the ability to critically examine them in terms of their validity to the client's PROBLEMS IN LIVING and what they might offer as ways of working with clients; the opportunity to identify strengths within particular theoretical approaches without having to 'swallow them whole'
- a commitment to personal and professional development throughout one's working career, starting with an ability to recognise strengths, ambitions and growth edges
- the ability to undertake a range of tasks associated with building an understanding of client needs and how to respond to them, including the ability to recognise one's own preferences and beliefs and where growth is most needed.

Cooper and McLeod (2011a) have identified three stages in formal training in pluralistic therapy that should structure programmes of study:

First stage: Development of generic COUNSELLING SKILLS and recognition of existing strengths and knowledge that may be employed in therapy; embedding an understanding of COMMON FACTORS and what is found to be helpful across modalities; tapping into the student's own experience of being helped or being helpful, and engaging in relational activities within the programme. A trainee at the end of this stage would have a good sense of their own capacity and growth edges.

Second stage: Learning to differentiate between methods used in helping relationships; developing the ability to respond to preferences and offer different ways of working – for example, being able to i) explore issues and create meaning, ii) structure change and problem-solving strategies, iii) activate client strengths and resources.

Third stage: Post-qualification, embark on a life-long journey to develop skills in particular areas of practice, either identified through personal reflection on gaps in their own skillset or adapting and improving an ability that is important for their work context.

At various points during the process of establishing themselves and working as a pluralistic therapist, it is helpful for a practitioner to articulate, discuss and defend their responses to the following questions around their own philosophy of therapy and personal knowledge:

- What sets of ideas provide the social, political and philosophical context for your theory of counselling?
- How do you understand the nature of humanness and personality?
- How do psychological/emotional/relationship problems develop?

- How do you account for the perpetuation of problems?
- How do you explain the process of therapeutic change?
- How do you understand the relationship between counsellor and client? What is the role of the relationship in facilitating learning and change?
- What therapeutic interventions are consistent (or inconsistent) with your model and why?
- What are the values outcomes of counselling? What are you trying to achieve?
- What evidence do you use to determine whether valued outcomes are being achieved?
- What is the direction of your theoretical development (what will you work towards understanding)?
- What are the unresolved theoretical issues that you wish to explore over the next few years?

Answering these questions will require a trainee to 'dig deep' into their own belief systems and structures and appreciate where these originate and how they influence their work with clients. They will also understand that each theoretical approach will have its own answers to these questions and recognise the multiplicity of 'truths' that exist. Each trainee and practitioner therapist will have their own answers, but so too will many clients; some truths will resonate with others, and some may be mutually exclusive.

Supervision and scope of practice

Broadly speaking, pluralistic supervision is no different from that used in other approaches to therapy. However, there are some key features that draw on the pluralistic principles to aid collaborative and creative supervisory relationships (Creamer & Timulak, 2016).

It is helpful for trainee pluralistic therapists to have a supervisor who holds an integrative stance. However, once they are qualified and confident to work with the PLURALISTIC

FRAMEWORK, it may be that supervision with a practitioner who works within a particular theoretical frame can present a developmental opportunity for a pluralistic therapist to understand and advance their theoretical range and introduce them to new methodologies that may be helpful for their clients. A supervisor may thus be tasked with taking a supervisory and oversight role, and that of an educator.

The supervisor of a pluralistic therapist may be required to work with some ideas that may be contrary to their own training and mode of working, such as:

- that there are many different ways that people can be helped, and that this implies that there are many change processes, many ways of knowing and 'both/and' ways of thinking
- that clients understand what is likely to be helpful/unhelpful for them, and some of the ways that the therapist will be working will privilege what the client has chosen as the best route.

Collaboration is the primary mode of being in a client-therapist relationship, and this is also true for supervisor-therapist relationships. Feedback and dialogue are used to keep the supervision focused on areas of relevance, and clarification is sought when needed. In many ways, the supervisory relationship can be a good model for the pluralistic therapy relationship, with opportunities for trial and error and mutuality within the process, and for the GOALS of the process to be articulated and set out in the supervision contract.

Currently there are relatively few pluralistic supervisors, so generic supervisors working with a pluralistic therapist should have a core understanding of the PLURALISTIC FRAMEWORK and ways of working and not simply an ability to understand the PLURALISTIC STANCE. The reason for this is that:

- therapists may be breaching the traditionally perceived boundaries with regard to what is and what is not included in the therapy process

- the therapist may be adapting and amending their understanding of the client's issues and how to deal with them in ways that are consistent with their understanding of a particular client but may be inconsistent across their clients
- methodological and theoretical purists may struggle to find the internal logic of what a therapist is doing and may have to seek an explanation based on the therapist's understanding of the client and their collaborative FORMULATION of the problem.

Some aspects of practice may be more prominent in pluralistic therapists than in those working from other integrative perspectives. These include an emphasis on the technical aspects of therapy, the METHODS and ways of undertaking different tasks with their clients, and an openness to understanding PROBLEMS IN LIVING from different theoretical perspectives. Finally, because pluralistic therapy requires a practitioner to respond to client need, the variety of ways of working and METHODS available to the therapist is always growing and evolving to allow a therapist to expand what they might offer from their therapeutic MENU. A pluralistic therapist will be actively engaged in lifelong personal and professional development and will be using supervision as a way of undertaking this, in addition to seeking learning opportunities and advice or recommendations for activities.

Common challenges in supervision

Some aspects of pluralistic therapy are more commonly experienced as challenging to therapists and so more likely to feature in supervision. These issues include the ability of the therapist to work effectively with client GOALS, or the concept of GOALS in general.

- Therapists can lose sight of what the client actually wants and focus more on what they are able and feel comfortable to offer, leading to a drift towards other activities or non-directional and purposeless dialogue, or feeling they

have a better understanding of client need than the client themselves.
- Some therapists struggle with the process of externalising a CASE FORMULATION and presenting the client with a written draft with their interpretations and suggestions. The barriers here tend to be that the therapist has concerns that the client will feel overwhelmed, that the information may be inaccurate or poorly presented, and that the presentation of the FORMULATION may create a power imbalance between the therapist and client. Supervision can help the therapist to present their FORMULATION in a way that is suitably speculative, as an honest account of what they are seeing, so that the client is able to accept it for what it is and express their opinion and resonance with the ideas presented. The therapist may wish to present their CASE FORMULATION to their supervisor as a rehearsal, giving the supervisor an opportunity to ask questions and use a stance of curiosity to help the therapist evolve their ideas.
- The therapist may slip into the expert position and fail to collaborate effectively with the client. Because pluralistic therapy is seen as more dialogic than many other approaches, and because the therapist is invited to own their knowledge and experience in collaboration with the client, it can sometimes be difficult to adjust this to meet the client's needs. The ability to monitor this and step back when it occurs relies on self-awareness, and the recognition of its impact on client work often occurs in supervision.
- The therapist may lose confidence or feel discomfort when faced with a client's distress and so rush to find solutions when what may be needed is patience and a capacity for tolerating uncertainty that allows for the unfolding of the therapeutic process.

Lifelong learning and deliberate practice

Because of the emphasis in pluralistic therapy on therapist knowledge and the open nature of its philosophy and possible ways of working with clients, practitioners are likely to be engaged in the development of therapeutic skills and knowledge throughout their lives. This life-long learning imperative allows therapists to evolve their practice in creative and personally meaningful ways. Effective therapists engage in ongoing personal and professional development and avoid losing touch with their sense of novice stress (Skovholt & Jennings, 2005).

Rousmaniere's deliberate practice (2016) provides pluralistic therapists with a focus for recognising and improving skills. It is useful to establish this as a therapist practice during training, but it may also be a skill that clients can use to undertake changes in behaviour or functioning. Deliberate practice involves the identification of aspects of therapeutic skill that need to be improved (for example, empathic reflection, helping clients to articulate GOALS and navigating shared decision-making) and, once these are identified, the practitioner creates opportunities for rehearsal or conscious testing to improve their skills (McLeod, 2021). This is ideally done in supervision or with peer-learners, using role-play.

Chapter 8
Common questions and answers

Pluralistic therapy is an approach that lends itself to discussion, debate and challenge. This chapter will explore and answer some of the questions commonly raised by critics and those considering the approach.

Q: Can you work in a single modality and have a pluralistic perspective?

A: Yes, as mentioned in Chapter 1, a therapist can work from a single modality if they are flexible, collaborative and able to adapt to a client's preferences within their existing model.

Or a therapist might adopt a PLURALISTIC STANCE (honouring the effectiveness of other modalities) while practising from a single perspective. This may mean that they are willing to hold a conversation with clients prior to therapy to allow them to make an informed choice about the therapy on offer and would certainly consider referring on if the client's needs would be better met elsewhere.

On the other hand, while pluralistic therapy aims to provide a structure and framework for cross-school applications of therapy, some aspects, such as therapist adaptation to client preferences, do not align to some theoretical approaches. So, for example, psychodynamic approaches see working with defence mechanisms and transference as central (Spurling, 2016), which might present a barrier to allowing the client's preferences to be privileged over the therapist's interpretations. Similarly, the actualising tendency is a fundamental 'truth' in person-centred therapy and central to its non-directive approach (Ong et al., 2020), whereas the pluralistic approach is based on the principle that there are no universal truths, which may be difficult, but not impossible, to reconcile (Cooper & McLeod, 2011b).

Q: Is pluralistic therapy actually just integration?

A: As explained in Chapter 1, INTEGRATION is used by most counselling and therapy practitioners even when they identify with a single school of therapy. It is how this INTEGRATION takes place that distinguishes the pluralistic and the integrative approaches. Pluralistic therapy is based on a humanistic ethical stance and a post-modern perspective. It is unique within the integrative field in providing a rationale for how problems in living are understood, a framework for the application of a wide range of therapies, and a set of principles that underpin how the pluralistic therapist works, including prioritisation of openness, collaboration and client choice and preference.

Q: How does pluralistic therapy position the therapist in relation to the balance of power in the therapy room?

A: The pluralistic approach rejects the notion of the therapist as having superior knowledge about the client's experience and thus how therapy is undertaken. This is attested by its principle of the primacy of the client, the positioning of the client as 'heroic', in its emphasis on collaboration and openness to feedback, and the manner in which the client's experiences are formulated according to their understanding of the world and their preferences for what is done about it. It is also shown by its use of the client's knowledge, the therapist's knowledge and common knowledge. Pluralistic therapists do not decide which information is used; rather, they bring their knowledge and experience about what may be therapeutically useful to the collaboration with the client.

Q: Are pluralistic therapists 'Jacks of all trades' (and masters/mistresses of none)?

A: This issue is often raised in relation to the training of pluralistic therapists, which is outlined in Chapter 7. A therapist can use the PLURALISTIC FRAMEWORK to respond to a breadth of client experience, so will need to be skilled in core COUNSELLING SKILLS and pluralistic competencies, such as structuring the collaborative process, garnering and responding to feedback, and tailoring what they do. They are less likely to hold advanced skills in one specialist area. Pluralistic therapy graduates are taught to continually review their developmental needs with the expectation of lifelong learning, and therapists who have training in a single modality and adopt the pluralistic approach will of course bring their existing skills to the work and be able to expand their skill-set in myriad ways.

Q: Is pluralistic therapy just another modality among many other modalities?

A: The pluralistic answer is both yes and no. Pluralistic therapy is rooted in humanistic values and assumptions, such as prizing diversity and individuality, and in practice it does require an alignment with the principles of pluralistic therapy outlined in Chapter 2. It has also been stressed that the theory of pluralistic therapy should be held lightly, in line with the pluralistic principle that there are no 'truths' (Cooper & McLeod, 2011a).

In order for pluralistic therapy to be considered monistic, it must have unique defining characteristics and specific ways of undertaking therapy. While pluralistic therapy would argue that it does have distinctive features (McLeod, 2018), these relate more to its fundamental humanistic and ethical stance rather than how it is practised (although the former influences the latter). What pluralistic therapy is suggesting to the field of counselling and psychotherapy is a different way of looking at therapy and making practice judgements based on an ethical stance and set of principles rather than a fixed modality or theoretical frame.

Q: Is my pluralistic therapy the same as your pluralistic therapy?

A: One of the features of pluralistic therapy is its ability to embrace difference and diversity in clients, and subsequently also diversity in practice. Therapists can be trained in pluralistic therapy as a specific way of working (Cooper & Dryden, 2016), or they can have diverse trainings in varied modalities and adopt pluralistic principles and work in a pluralistic way.

Therapists are individual and will develop unique and idiosyncratic ways of responding to clients that will also be influenced by the client's responses in an interactive, relational process. Therapists have unique sets of common and personal knowledge and resources and these, and their unique personalities, will inform and shape their practice, so how they practice will and should look different. Pluralistic therapists are metaphorically artists or *bricoleurs* and, in the same way that no two works of art will ever be the same, nor will pluralistic practice.

Q: Does pluralistic therapy offer something for everyone?

A: Pluralistic practice is not for everyone; many people (therapists and clients) feel more comfortable in a world of truths. Single modality approaches can provide firm boundaries around what should and should not be done in therapy, with clear guidelines underpinned by distinct theories and robust research about the causes of problems and what resolves them. Even pluralistic therapists will have areas of therapeutic activity that they either do not feel competent to undertake or that do not sit well with their understanding of the problem or the client. It may be that the flexibility of the approach means that it will have a broad appeal and applicability to any client. In theory, far more client needs can be accommodated by meeting the client where they are, rather than where theory needs them to be, and by the flexibility of the pluralistic approach, which allows helpful METHODS to be drawn from a wider range of sources and applied creatively. However, the comparative effectiveness of this approach is not yet empirically established by research (see Chapter 9).

Q: Isn't the framework a bit prescriptive?

A: The pluralistic nested hierarchy of TASKS within GOALS can be taken too literally. Rather than using this as an opportunity for meaning-making and creativity, therapists and clients can become distracted by the idea that they are looking for something that already exists out there. A TASK is simply an event, activity or process that needs to happen in order to progress towards a GOAL, and may be aligned to the processes of directionality: for example, 'discovering', 'recognising', 'determining', 'deciding', 'understanding', 'planning', 'acting' and 'instilling' are all action-based TASK definers. METHODS, which are often confused with TASKS, are the actions themselves – how a TASK is addressed. For example, in order to recognise and understand the impact of a mother's behaviour on a client (the TASK), the client and therapist may wish to create a reflective space to explore the events by talking things through (METHOD), or they may use metaphors (METHOD) that represent and deepen unexplored ideas. There will be times in the therapy when the task at hand is not clear and the therapist and client decide to try an activity to see what comes up. Conceptually, the task here might be simply to let something emerge. This is described in a little more detail in Chapter 5.

The use of GOALS has also been seen by some as unhelpfully outcome-oriented. However, even the most non-directive therapist will surely agree that, in order for a client to experience change, they must take a step from where they are to where they end up as a result of therapy. Across the pluralistic field, the use of GOALS ranges from 'SMART' targeting and measuring outcomes to simply having a sense of movement and direction that is meaningful for the client. The key point is that the therapist and client talk about what the client wants or expects from therapy and agree how this will shape their choice of activities.

Q: What about therapies that go beyond talking?

A: The pluralistic approach is by definition open to the use of a range of techniques, including non-verbal and arts-based therapies. Recently, for example, there has been a development in the field for a pluralistic arts-based therapeutic approach for working with depression (Parsons, et al., 2020, 2021).

Simply engaging in art in therapy, or in EXTRA-THERAPY ACTIVITIES, can be beneficial for mental and physical health (Stuckey & Nobel, 2010). There are many different theories and techniques that can be drawn upon, including projective techniques where problems or internal conflicts are 'projected' into the art or activity, such as painting or sand-tray work, for example.

Creative METHODS can be particularly valuable for some clients when working with problems that are hard to express or explain in words, for example. Non-verbal activities, such as art, play or movement, can help the client process highly charged emotions and experiences when words cannot be found (Silverstone, 1997), which can facilitate meaning-making and the creation of new narratives.

Not all pluralistic therapists or clients will want to work with creative METHODS, and there are risks as well as benefits. Clients may respond in unexpected and very visceral ways; emotions can surface quickly and intensely, and some clients may feel overwhelmed (Springham, 2008). The key to working with creative METHODS in pluralistic practice is to do so collaboratively and with a clear rationale.

Q: Where next for pluralistic therapy?

A: Pluralistic therapy is growing in popularity and the ways in which it is used are changing. Online therapy is far more common than in recent years and may be an ideal platform for pluralistic therapy because it offers a different range of ways of interacting from which the client can choose to suit their individual needs and preferences. It is also, arguably, a platform congruent with the pluralistic emphasis on GOALS, TASKS and the importance of feedback (Berger, 2017; Cipolletta et al., 2018; Geller, 2020).

Group therapy and personal development groups in counsellor training have already been adapted for pluralistic training across a number of institutions, including exploration of group-based GOALS, TASKS and METHODS, the COLLABORATIVE RELATIONSHIP, multiple perspectives and use of process monitoring and feedback.

Chapter 9
Research on pluralistic therapy

Given that pluralistic therapy is aligned to the humanistic belief that ideas are not truths, the search for empirical evidence to support practice could be considered a moral and philosophical imperative. However, there is a notable absence of research evidence across counselling and psychotherapy, and pluralistic therapy is no different.

The research relating to pluralistic therapy can be grouped under three broad headings: the research evidence that underpins the principles of the pluralistic approach, and led to the development of, and continues to influence, the PLURALISTIC FRAMEWORK; research into the process, experience and outcome of pluralistic therapy, and the pluralistic therapy literature more generally on how it will move forward with the research and evidence-based agenda.

Developmental and underpinning research evidence

While broad-based outcome studies of PLURALISTIC PRACTICE have not yet been undertaken, it is supported by several lines of research. Generic and specific aspects of the framework, including collaborative information-sharing, SHARED DECISION-MAKING, flexibility and embedded feedback systems are all supported by empirical research (Bohart & Tallman, 1999). There is also evidence that improved outcomes and reduced drop-out rates result when the therapy methods are aligned to the client's wishes (Handelzalts & Keinan, 2010; Lindhiem et al., 2014; Swift et al., 2018), and that clients know what works for them and are likely to seek it in therapy (Cooper, 2008; Kühnlein, 1999). SHARED DECISION-MAKING is also shown to reduce client dropout (Joosten et al., 2009; Health Foundation, 2013).

Collaboration within a strong relationship characterised by shared striving towards agreed therapeutic GOALS using agreed METHODS is associated with positive outcomes (Horvath et al., 2011; Tryon & Winograd, 2011). Use of structured feedback systems has also been found to enhance outcome for clients, particularly when they are at risk of deterioration or dropout (Lambert & Shimokawa, 2011). Clients report that it is helpful when their feedback is used to inform the therapy process (Antoniou et al., 2017). Underlining this is the finding that therapists and clients only agree on what is significant in therapy in 30–40% of events (Cummings et al., 1992; Martin & Stelmaczonek, 1988; Timulak, 2010), and that clients are more likely to defer to the therapist, with a resulting decrease in effectiveness (Rennie, 1994). There is also evidence that therapist preferences may not reflect those of their clients (Cooper et al., 2019).

Ethically, PLURALISTIC PRACTICE seeks to aid clients by offering them what they find most helpful, and in practice what is helpful tends to be unique to the client (and a bit unpredictable). Research has produced a huge bank of data on what clients consider important, impactful and helpful in therapy (e.g. Elliott, 1985; McLeod, 2012; Timulak, 2007). They include cross-theoretical factors characterised by 'helpfulness', and relational factors such as reassurance, feeling understood, and personal contact (Timulak, 2010). All of this supports the less SCHOOLIST approach of pluralistic therapy. There is also evidence that clients experience flexible practice tailored to their individual, complex and multidimensional needs (McLeod, 2012) as a helpful and important aspect of therapy (Antoniou et al., 2017; Cooper et al., 2015; Perren et al., 2009). This too is linked to improved outcomes and greater engagement with therapy.

Research into the process, experience and outcomes of pluralistic therapy

The pluralistic approach is, of course, relatively new and so the evidence base for its application is only just emerging. In terms of comparative effectiveness and outcomes, it has been shown to be effective in a multi-site trial with clients living with depression, with good results for retention and outcomes: more than 90% of clients engaged for two sessions or more, and there was an effect size of 1.83 on the primary outcome measure (PHQ-9) (Cooper et al., 2015). The development of a competencies scale to examine the adherence of practitioners to the approach is likely to bring about an increase in evidence for outcomes in therapy.

As mentioned, the emphasis in PLURALISTIC PRACTICE on what the client finds useful in therapy has formed the basis of research into client experiences and preferences: for example, the use of feedback forms (Bowen & Cooper, 2012), helpful events (Watson et al., 2012) and preferences (McLeod, 2012; Walls et al., 2016), where the client voice is privileged over the researcher's and therapist's ideas and assumptions. Walls and colleagues (2016) applied a PLURALISTIC FRAME to the question of client preference at a counselling service for people with alcohol problems. When asked, clients expressed preferences and provided a reason for those preferences and also demonstrated an openness to other ideas about what might be helpful.

They also tended to have some preferences for aspects of therapy that would not normally be considered in a counselling service, such as being given advice and for the counsellor to share their own life-experiences and perspectives. This wish to know more about the counsellor appeared to be linked to a concern about being judged (common in people with addiction problems), which was countered by respectful collaboration. The participants also flagged up an interest in EXTRA-THERAPY RESOURCES, but only ones that suited them. Preferences for the focus of the therapy ranged widely, with some finding consideration of the cause and background of their problem to be helpful while others said they preferred not to dwell on the past. A key finding was that, in this population, where drop-out is known to be a significant problem, aligning to preference may be the best way to develop the therapeutic relationship.

The application of pluralistic therapy was also examined by Miller and Willig (2012) in a qualitative study of HIV-positive clients. This study highlighted the importance of the shared knowledge of the client and therapist. This was reported as fundamental to a sense that the therapist's understanding of the client was built from their knowledge of the individual and their experience, rather than derived from a particular theoretical model. The study also identified an appreciation that sessions could be client-led, with the idea that 'two therapists are better than one'; clients felt better able to respond to challenge because they felt they knew where the therapist was coming from. Clients also appreciated the openness of the therapists' approach: that they worked to open up and hold a space for exploration, but also helped identify existing resources and 'pooled information' with the client.

The course of pluralistic therapy does not follow a standard pattern and examining the outcomes and processes therefore requires the use of research methodologies that are capable of capturing that complexity. The suitability of systematic case studies to evidence the unique and nuanced nature of a pluralistic approach to therapy and how it can be applied through a single therapeutic frame is demonstrated by McLeod (2013) in her research into the use of transactional analysis for people living with long-term health conditions. This research used transcripts, client reports and outcome measures to identify TASKS that were categorised as insight- and meaning-making (for example, resolving past events to help with current and future wellbeing), self-perspective activities (for example, addressing the sense of worthlessness), and practical activities (for example, coping strategies and pain management techniques). The emerging understandings from this kind of work are vital to the pluralistic approach because they triangulate data sets while remaining very closely aligned with client experience in therapy. Thurston (2016) also used the close reading of case-study data to produce her influential work on developing a pluralistic approach to counselling for sight loss.

Beyond McLeod's work (2013), there is limited research into the application of a pluralistic approach using interventions from a single modality. Utry and colleagues (2015) have examined the potential role of the pluralistic approach in coaching and concluded that the principles of SHARED DECISION-MAKING and collaboration are likely to enhance effectiveness. However this, like many of the proposals for how the pluralistic approach works, has not been empirically tested. This boundary between the integrative and single-modality use of the pluralistic approach is likely to grow as the approach develops as a transtheoretical frame.

Moving forward with the research and evidence-based agenda

It has been suggested that pluralistic researchers should adopt a pluralistic approach to examining (i.e. reading and interpreting) and undertaking research (Cooper & McLeod, 2007, 2011a; Hanley & Winter, 2016). This suggestion takes the notion that all truths can be accommodated in therapy and applies it to research. Within this, it is also proposed that the research methodology should align to the question being asked (a little like linking the METHOD to the TASK and GOAL of therapy). This pluralistic philosophy influences the approach the movement takes towards the ontology and epistemology – namely, what is and what can be examined and understood and how.

In some respects, the question 'Does it work?' requires studies that view the application of the pluralistic approach as a 'way of doing therapy'. In other words, research evidencing effectiveness would need to evaluate interventions aligned to specific competencies and activities, such as active engagement in feedback, and whether this results in positive outcomes for clients (while allowing the methods used within this frame to be wide ranging). This could be complemented by research that examines the complexity of the approach, rather than the interventions themselves, in a holistic sense. Some theoretical discussion has challenged the over-reliance on causality in research, arguing that the tradition of measurable and delineated cause-and-effect relationships, such as 'Does the application of six sessions of therapy reduce symptoms of depression in adults?', can stifle opportunities for gaining understanding. Using Denzin's (2006; 2012) process of triangulation of data, theory and methodological and researcher stance, it may be that a broad landscape of research projects using different methods and approaches will provide a rich evidence base for pluralistic therapy. This is based on the need to understand not simply the outcomes of therapy but also its impact on lived experience.

Going forward, a focus on initiatives that are directly related to practice and questions that are about what is important to know or understand will hopefully decrease the gap between research and practice in pluralistic therapy. The pluralistic approach is likely to prioritise research by level of relevance, population, group or individual, intervention, experience or outcome, and ask 'To whom is this information important?'

The use of research evidence in practice draws on empirical research, observations, case studies, reports and personal and professional interpretation of experiences and outcomes. So, in order to have an influence on therapy practice and engage practitioners, the pluralistic approach is interested in how to make research more reflective of therapy, more relevant and accessible to practitioners, and more co-creative. This may include the use of practitioner networks to generate discussion and debate and bringing together academics, practitioners and clients in collaborative research. Research that involves all the stakeholders in a collaborative partnership will result in meaningful co-creation rather than tokenistic inclusion (Greenhalgh et al., 2016), which sits comfortably with the pluralistic philosophy as it invites multiple truths and perspectives.

Outstanding questions

There are many important questions about pluralistic therapy that are yet to be answered. More evidence is needed on the effectiveness of the approach, both to support its use and also to inform its improvement and direction of development and growth. The first step will be to ask whether the research-based assumptions that led to the creation of the framework are well-founded. For example, the evidence points to the role of the collaborative relationship in both improving outcomes and reducing drop-out; in practice, is there a correlation between these when the emphasis on collaboration is articulated and explicit? In terms of the application and process of pluralistic therapy, important research questions include, what are the most meaningful outcomes for clients? How important do they rate having their preferences met, and how helpful is it when therapists adopt methods that fit to client preferences and needs? How can this responsiveness be enhanced and what are the primary factors in creating effective collaboration during experiences of distress and chronic disempowerment? Drilling down into these issues will allow detailed examination of what activities and actions are most effective, for whom and in what circumstances.

A further essential question is how the principle of equality can be best enacted through therapy. An important future focus of research is to explore the credibility of the approach in expanding equality and inclusivity. Research could examine how marginalised groups experience pluralistic therapy in practice, and how it can be used to better meet the needs of individuals where power imbalances are more prevalent and impactful. It would also be helpful to examine how non-European theories and modalities can be adopted to expand the options for change.

Some examples of postgraduate research questions include:

- How do clients define GOALS before and during therapy and how well matched are the therapeutic TASKS to their attainment in pluralistic therapy?
- How can pluralistic therapists best respond to minority groups?
- What are the challenges to the sharing of power and collaborative working for chronically disempowered clients

(e.g. residential mental health service users, those living in prison)?

- How do single modality pluralists enact the principles of the approach?

Chapter 10
Case study

The following case study illustrates some of the key features of the pluralistic approach. The study is of one client only, to help the reader get a sense of the application of the framework. However, because of its very nature, a pluralistic approach with one client will have a range of features, including GOALS, TASKS, METHODS and relational characteristics that will be very different from any other. In order to emphasise the primacy of the client voice, Maddy's view of the therapy is depicted here, rather than a theoretical interpretation. Maddy is fictitious but aspects of the case are drawn from client work at the research clinic at Abertay University. In the description of the process of therapy, the comments in bold type are used to highlight specific aspects of pluralistic practice.

The client

Maddy is 29 years old, female, the mother of one son, Asif, who is eight years old. She shares parental responsibilities with his father, Nadeem, but she and Nadeem no longer live together. She has a part-time job as a receptionist at a local housing association and is studying part-time towards a degree in psychology.

She was referred to the research clinic attached to her university counselling service by her GP because she had been experiencing low mood, feeling stressed and anxious, and was finding it increasingly hard to moderate her behaviour towards her son. Asif had recently moved schools as a result of his behaviour, and had been diagnosed with autism. Maddy had found both the diagnosis and her son's behaviour a concern, and felt she was not able to cope with his emotional outbursts and anger. She felt he was rejecting her and was also concerned that she did not respond well to him. She felt restricted by his need for regularity and control in his life.

Maddy was not brought up in a particular religion but adopted Islam shortly after meeting and marrying Nadeem in her late teens. She has retained her engagement with her Mosque after the breakdown of the relationship but feels she has more recently drifted from the faith. Both she and Nadeem are keen for Asif to be part of the local religious community.

Maddy describes her childhood as 'bog standard'. She grew up in a small town and talks about her teenage years as involving 'lots of shagging' and 'lots of fun' until she fell in love with Nadeem, who was living locally for his studies. He grew up in the city and, when they married, Maddy went to live within his extended family community, with whom she still has good connections now she has moved into her own home.

The therapist

Sally is a white British female in her mid-50s. She worked in teaching for 20 years, then retrained as a pluralistic therapist in her 40s and has more than 10 years' postgraduate experience with clients. She works in the university counselling service and volunteers at the research clinic where Maddy has been referred. Sally works in a flexible and highly collaborative way with her clients. She tends to draw on her generic COUNSELLING SKILLS and her training in psychodynamic, person-centred and narrative approaches. With Maddy, she drew mainly on the narrative approach, using letter-writing and life-story work. Sally is agnostic and explored Maddy's sense of her own spirituality from an enquiring and naïve stance.

Formulation and goals

The research clinic was able to offer Maddy 24 free sessions of therapy. In the first few sessions, Sally invited Maddy to discuss her GOALS for therapy. Maddy said she had a fairly good idea of what counselling involved, and she was able to engage in the co-creation of a TIMELINE FORMULATION in sessions 2 and 3. She felt that she would benefit most in the first stage of therapy by exploring why she felt she was not performing as a mother. She wanted to talk it over and see what came up. As the therapy progressed, she increasingly worked on her own sense of identity, her response to the circumstances she found herself in, and her ability to seek fulfilment for herself – to be happier, less stressed and more content and accepting of her life while she held things in place for her son. Sally and Maddy adopted a metaphor of a shopping centre to frame the choices that Maddy could make about activities: going into shops, trying things on (METHODS) and buying her favourite clothes, knowing what she was shopping for (TASKS) and knowing why she needed things (GOALS).

TASK – Getting to know who she is and what she wants (primarily sessions 1–6)

This TASK involved an exploration of how and why Maddy felt a tension between what was expected of her and her own desire for freedom and release. Sally used open, reflective talking and inquiry about her emotional experiences to encourage Maddy to express her frustration and distress at her current situation and her feeling that time was passing by and that she had limited choices. Maddy was able to look at her conflicting responsibilities and start to recognise and make sense of the challenges presented by her current experience to her hopes for the future. This lessened the feelings of stress and anxiety associated with them. From session 5, Maddy started to generate ideas and try out ways of making space for her own needs, which included re-engaging with her religious practice – a resource she had valued and had disengaged from.

The work focused for three sessions on the variety and difference between the ways that Maddy presented in the world. Sally and Maddy used their experience of this sense of plural identities to identify Maddy's various life-roles (e.g. Maddy the mum; Maddy the good wife). Maddy revealed that she had another secret identity: 'Maddy the goddess'. She introduced her in quite a playful way, both making a joke of it but also being quite serious about there being this other person who she could be. Sally picked up on this identity by being interested and validating Maddy's need to tap into what felt like a powerful aspect of her self-image.

Sally maintained an accepting space where Maddy felt free to choose who she was. Maddy's feeling was that she liked that her varied roles would remain separate but that, if the time was right, and with the right person, she would like them to merge. She felt that 'Maddy the mum' was the role she spent most time in but it was also the one that took over the others and so needed monitoring. Her awareness of the roles she undertook was enhanced by Sally recognising and reflecting how she herself responded differently to Maddy in her different roles.

TASK – Re-engaging with Maddy's spiritual beliefs (session 5–10)
Maddy used the therapeutic space to discuss how she might re-engage with her Muslim community as an EXTRA-THERAPY RESOURCE, and this also led to her ongoing exploration of her understanding of religion and belief systems as not just a structure of faith but a way of making sense of her existence. The exploration of the nature of her religious beliefs and the ability to hold them lightly – sensing Allah as benign and forgiving in allowing her to keep faith while remaining relatively non-observant – recurred frequently in therapy sessions. Sally acknowledged her own agnosticism and they used this difference as a way to discuss the sense of purpose that Maddy's beliefs gave her. Through this, Maddy was able to reach a conceptualisation of her own life being different from any 'after life', which meant she felt able to make active choices.

TASK – Making space for Maddy the goddess (session 9–13)
Sally and Maddy returned to the identity work in session 9. Maddy was able to compare her current sense of self with that of the pre-marriage Maddy. Sally used her own observations of Maddy and

her experience of being in the therapy relationship to help her understand how Maddy might be responding. For example, Sally reflected that she noticed Maddy tended to change the subject when Sally referred to her (Maddy's) own needs, as though she felt it was 'self-indulgent' to explore what she might like from life. Sally said she felt a strong sense of sadness when this happened. Sally also remarked on differences in Maddy's demeanour when she was speaking as a mother and when she was speaking from her 'younger self'. She said it resonated with her own life roles and that sometimes it was as if they were two mothers talking, and that when the younger Maddy was talking, she felt more maternal towards her.

Maddy had buried 'Maddy the goddess' under the other roles that she had adopted of wife and mother. Having chosen to go back and explore her 'pre-marriage' life on the timeline, Maddy realised that Maddy the goddess was valuable to her. She recognised the tensions between this role and her love for her son when Sally reflected that the two roles rarely came up in the same sessions, and this led them to look at how she could be both Maddy the goddess and Maddy the mum. This involved her accepting who her son was, rather than resisting it as it wasn't how she wanted him to be, and also accepting that she, in the role of mother, was not so vital to his wellbeing.

Getting in touch with her sexual desires and needs was essential for Maddy the goddess and for opening the opportunity for new relationships. A barrier to her acknowledging these was that they represented an aspect of life that she felt did not fit with everything else she was doing. Sally suggested that, if Maddy found it hard to talk about her sexuality in therapy, perhaps she could express it in writing. Maddy didn't think this would work, but the suggestion catalysed a conversation where she recognised that the absence of sexual release could be feeding her stress and low mood. Maddy recognised that her physical experience was very important to her sense of who she was and her own wellbeing; that she felt romantically and sexually frustrated by her current circumstances. Sally validated these ideas and they worked on visualisation and embodied work to support Maddy to articulate her desires and link these to her sense of being held back or stuck. Maddy learned from this experience to be more sensitive to her needs to express herself sexually and to allow herself to be open to romantic and sexual encounters.

Process monitoring and feedback

Alongside an open and collaborative stance in conversation with Maddy, Sally used process monitoring tools in the form of GOALS forms, session reviews based on the helpful aspects of therapy, C-NIP (Cooper & Norcross, 2016) and CORE (Evans et al., 2000).

Outcomes and the use of process monitoring

Sally used weekly CORE-OM measures to monitor Maddy's mood throughout the therapy. In session 2, Maddy had said she felt so depressed that she would be considered 'at risk', and the CORE-OM measures appeared to corroborate this. Maddy said she was taking significant periods of time off work, ostensibly to care for her son but in fact she spent these days in bed, crying. The presence of risk in the therapeutic collaboration raised the question of whether and when Sally would need to raise a concern about Maddy's safety, and became part of the collaboration in the early stages.

Sally asked Maddy how she might like her to manage any concerns if they arose: should she flag them at the time or at the end of the session, and how would these impact on Maddy's sense of choice? Maddy said she would like to know 'how bad' it looked from Sally's perspective, but that she would also like to get a better sense of how these judgements were made. What would trigger Sally's concern enough to prompt her to contact Maddy's GP, as agreed? This led to some psychoeducation, as Sally shared her knowledge and experience of working with suicide risk. This shared responsibility for risk monitoring decreased over the course of therapy, but the conversation helped Maddy with her empowerment and sense of validation. So while, overall, the management of risk drew on therapist knowledge around risk, it also involved Sally sharing this knowledge and the SHARED DECISION-MAKING around how to manage it.

Maddy's GOALS changed over the course of the therapy, but always related to re-establishing a life that would work for both her and her son. By the end of the therapy, Maddy had re-adjusted her ways of thinking about her role in her son's life and her religious beliefs and practices, and also felt empowered to recognise her sense of sexuality through the articulation of her identity and how this influenced her behaviour and judgements of herself. These outcomes were not always clear during the therapy but, by session 17, when Maddy decided to no longer attend sessions with Sally, both of them were able to track the journey they had shared and where it had ended up. Maddy no longer felt that her life had no meaning, and her mood and her ability to find meaning in her life and reprioritise her actions when she wanted and needed to had all improved. She also felt better able to navigate relationships with her son, ex-husband and potential new partners.

Maddy's case is both unique and typically pluralistic, in that the close collaboration between Sally and Maddy became a forum for creative and responsive working, for expression of emotion and meaning-making, for planning and negotiating life-changes, for recognising achievements, and for Maddy to renew her sense of purpose and regain her ability to move forward in a way that felt right for her and her family.

Table 10.1: Session monitoring and feedback

Session number	Helpful aspects *Unhelpful aspects (in the client's words)	Therapy relationship	CORE
1	'Just getting it off my chest' 'Feeling relieved that Sally was nice'	C-NIP indicated clear preferences for: i) encouraging difficult emotions ii) letting client take the lead iii) help understanding iv) be warm and informal	64 R=8

2	'Just talking about how depressed I am about being a mother'		50 R=5
3	'The time-line and the pens' 'Sally asking what I wanted felt like the first time I got a choice in a long time'		56 R=7
4	'Not keen on assuming my parents got it wrong when they raised me'*		30 R=1
5	'Talking about how counselling will work for me' 'Going shopping!' 'Sally understanding how hard it is to have an autistic son'		46 R=1
6	'Thinking why there has been a change in my mood'	C-NIP review indicated preferences for: i) focusing on adult experience and future ii) keeping a loose structure	38 R=0
7	'Talking about Allah without feeling guilty' 'Felt love, which is missing'		32 R=1
8	'Planning how to get back in touch with friends'		23 R=0

9	'Talking about sex and feeling horny – Sally helped me accept that my body is telling me something important'		22 R=0
10	'Felt a bit judged when I talked about dating'*		
11	'Talking about Maddy the goddess and dating' 'Talking about feeling judged'		24 R=0
12	'Sally reminding me that I love my son and he loves me' 'Helped me see that I can grow at the same time as him'		22 R=0
13	'Writing the letter to Asif and telling Sally about it, then creating a permission list' 'Discussing setbacks and feeling judged'	C-NIP discussed, not completed – conversation about the opportunity to discuss the therapeutic relationship	40 R=0
14	'Talking about how Sally and I interact and how she sees me'		34 R=0
15	'Talking about what it is like to be me in therapy' 'Sally reminding me what I find difficult in relationships'		14 R=0

16	'Mapping the future helped me see the changes' 'Telling Sally about Sol'		20 R=0
17	'Just happy to have got here – Thank you'		26 R=0

When the research clinic interviewed Maddy three months after the therapy ended, she was asked about her suicidal thoughts and how the therapy might have helped with these. Her comments indicate the ways in which an umbrella term such as 'depression', or even the idea of 'risk', is highly nuanced and experienced by the client in very personal terms.

> I needed some reason to be alive. I think the only thing that really mattered was Asif and, while that was true, he was also the centre of my daily stress. I was so frustrated by it all and I think I bottled it up and became paralysed. I was just pretending to be myself without really feeling anything. Somewhere along the line, I had forgotten how to feel happy, and when I had space to think about it, I just couldn't stop crying, like I would fall over the edge into a big black pit. I hadn't realised how bad it can get when you just try and keep going.

[Close attention to the way a client describes or interprets their experience can be used to develop a shared understanding and FORMULATION without being prescriptive about what might be done.]

When asked about the process of change she had undergone, Maddy reported that the work had helped her find aspects of her own identity that were being ignored or suppressed. She was able to say what Sally did to help:

> When Sally recognised that I rely on being sexy or feeling sexy to validate who I am, that really helped me understand what was going on for me. She helped me

see how this has been a bit stunted, actually locked up, for ages, since I was separated really. She helped me recognise my life-force as a strength

[A pluralistic therapist may provide interpretation or ideas to aid a client's understanding of themselves.]

Maddy was also able to understand her previous behaviour better, and use this meaning-making process to inform what she wanted to do next:

> I tended to flirt like mad with Nadeem. I realised I was doing this because I could get my kicks from feeling desirable but also he was safe enough to know that it wasn't going anywhere. I started to recognise that I was really worried that, if I let myself get back to dating, then I would risk Asif's stable home, and this would be a disaster.

[Developing insight is often the focus in the first stage of therapy, but is important throughout.]

Therapy also gave Maddy an opportunity to make changes in her life at a pace that suited her:

> So gradually getting back to it was a really important process. I had to feel safe and in control but also that I can do what I want with my own body. I am dating someone now, but being careful about how much time I give him, and being very aware of it not taking over my life (even when sometimes I want it to).

[Ultimately therapy is about the client getting to a place where they feel empowered to make choices and take actions according to their own wants and needs.]

Therapy also allowed Maddy space to explore her beliefs and religion in a way that helped her re-engage with something that was restorative and spiritually meaningful to her. Having this conversation in a safe space also helped her address a potential conflict in her life – being a good Muslim and being Maddy the goddess.

> It helps that I can make choices about my relationship with Allah and chatting with my online Muslim women's group is really helping to remind me what it is all about. There's sexism in all religions and you have to kind of tease out what is written and how it is interpreted. My Allah wants women to be bold.

[Tapping into EXTRA-THERAPY RESOURCES is essential to recognise that therapy is only one of the things that might help the client. They also serve as ongoing aspects of the client's life – in Maddy's case, her religious beliefs and her development of her relationship with Allah.]

The clinic asks all clients for sessional feedback, and Maddy was also asked in the follow-up interview to talk about anything Sally had done that was specifically helpful.

> We did some stuff around Sally helping me recognise the emotions I was feeling and allow myself to feel them. From this, I kind of understand the way I think I should be and the way that I want to be, like I was trying to fit a mould that doesn't suit me. We talked a lot about trying on outfits to see what suited me – actually, the whole shopping metaphor worked for us. It let me kind of try stuff out, or say, 'Hmm, not that shop today, let's go look somewhere else.' Overall, I know she saw something positive in me. She recognised my strengths and helped me trust them, I know she believes in me... actually we believe in each other.

[A pluralistic therapist will work to aid a client's active engagement in therapy and using metaphor can be helpful when thinking about this process. Pluralistic therapists will display a fundamental positive regard, allowing the client to recognise their own strengths.]

Maddy also indicated one of the activities undertaken at Sally's suggestion that was helpful to her:

> Sally asked me to write a letter to Azim to try and explain how I was feeling about him, about being his mum. It shook me, how hard it was to be honest with myself. From that I think I got in touch with what needed to change, and Sally encouraged me to give permission to myself. We had a whole session on my 'new rules' for myself and they are still stuck to the fridge.

[Using a range of METHODS *is an important aspect of the pluralistic approach that allows the therapist to mould the therapeutic activities to client need. This example demonstrates two forms of writing: the first, to explore and gain insight, and the second to support a change in the way the client thinks and behaves.]*

Asked about aspects of the therapy that were unhelpful, Maddy was able to identify some that were not to her liking but was confident that she had aired these concerns with Sally at the time:

> We had a bit of a bump when I felt that Sally didn't approve of my going on Tinder. I felt really positive about it when I told her. I was, like, 'solved the issue' but she looked really shocked. I told her how she looked but we sorted through that and I think it was a combination of her shock and my feeling judged, even when maybe it was me who was doing the judging. Anyway, she kind of explained her reaction. She said she hadn't really understood my readiness and the need. Plus, she said she was probably being old-fashioned, which is fine. She was honest and that was important, because I was being so open with her by that point, it helped to know she was being honest with me.

[At times all therapists make mistakes – it is how they acknowledge and return from them that is important.]

Maddy's case is an example of how a client can enter therapy with multiple, intertwining PROBLEMS IN LIVING and, through careful work identifying and validating strengths and desires, is able to develop new understandings of self and ways of being. In practice, the process involves flexibility, adaptability and creativity on the part of the client and counsellor. For Maddy, Sally's role was that of collaborator in therapy: both caring and fallible, but also combining her own skills and knowledge with Maddy's to engage in activities and use METHODS suited to Maddy's preferences and desired outcomes.

Appendix 1
Resources for learning

Online resources

www.pluralisticpractice.com – the main community hub for people working in pluralism, with links to courses, research and CPD, including:

- https://pluralisticpractice.com/tools-and-measures/ – process monitoring and feedback tools
- https://pluralisticpractice.com/blog/ – a guest-writer blogspot for commentary on pluralism in therapy and society more generally
- https://pluralisticpractice.com/training/ – training opportunities for anyone wishing to know more, incorporate a pluralistic stance, or train in the pluralistic framework.

The Pluralistic Approach to Counselling and Psychotherapy – an introductory video by Professor Mick Cooper of Roehampton University, one of its leading theorists, practitioners and advocates. Includes interviews, lectures, discussions and presentations.

www.bing.com/videos search?q=youtube+pluralistic+approach&docid=608031696130475220&mid=505A01267CDA4954A5AF505A01267CDA4954A5AF&view=detail&FORM=VIRE

https://mick-cooper.squarespace.com/pluralistic-therapy – Professor Mick Cooper's training and consultancy website, with links to relevant publications and several videos on the approach.

Recommended reading

General theory and practice

Cooper, M. & Dryden, W. (Eds.). (2016). *Handbook of pluralistic counselling and psychotherapy*. Sage.

Cooper, M., & Dryden, W. (2016). Introduction to pluralistic counselling and psychotherapy. In M. Cooper & W. Dryden (Eds.), *Handbook of pluralistic counselling and psychotherapy*. Sage.

Cooper, M., & McLeod, J. (2007). A pluralistic framework for counselling and psychotherapy: Implications for research. *Counselling and Psychotherapy Research 7*(3), 135–143. doi: 10.1080/14733140701566282

Cooper, M., & McLeod, J. (2010). Pluralism: Towards a new paradigm for therapy. *Therapy Today, 21*(9), 10–14.

Cooper, M., & McLeod, J. (2011). *Pluralistic counselling and psychotherapy*. London: Sage.

Cooper, M., & McLeod, J. (2012). From either/or to both/and: Developing a pluralistic approach to counselling and psychotherapy. *European Journal of Psychotherapy and Counselling, 14*(1), 5–18.

Hanley, T., Winter, L., McLeod, J., & Cooper, M. (2017). Pluralistic counselling psychology. In D. Murphy (Ed.), *Counselling psychology: A textbook for study and practice* (pp. 134–149). Wiley.

McLeod, J. (2013). Developing pluralistic practice in counselling and psychotherapy: Using what the client knows. *The European Journal of Counselling Psychology, 2*(1), 51–64.

McLeod, J. (2018). *Pluralistic therapy: Distinctive features*. Routledge.

McLeod, J., & Cooper, M. (2012). Pluralistic counselling and psychotherapy. In C. Feltham & I. Horton (Eds.), *The Sage handbook of counselling and psychotherapy* (pp. 368–371). Sage.

McLeod, J., & Cooper, M. (2015). Pluralistic counselling and psychotherapy. In S. Palmer (Ed.), *The beginner's guide to counselling and psychotherapy* (2nd ed) (pp. 322–332). Sage.

McLeod, J., McLeod, J., Cooper, M. & Dryden, W. (2014). Pluralistic therapy. In W. Dryden & A. Reeves (Eds.), *Handbook of individual therapy* (6th ed.) (pp. 547–573). Sage.

Client strengths and resources

Bohart, A.C., Tallman, K. (1999). *How clients make therapy work: The process of active self-healing*. American Psychological Association.

Duncan, B.L., Miller, S.D. & Sparks, J.A. (2004). *The heroic client: A revolutionary way to improve effectiveness through client-directed, outcome-informed therapy.* Wiley.

McLeod, J. (2018). Cultural resources. In J. McLeod, *Pluralistic therapy: Distinctive features* (pp.107–110). Routledge.

Appendix 2
Cooper–Norcross Inventory of Preferences (C-NIP) v1.1

On each of the items below, please indicate your preferences for how a psychotherapist or counsellor should work with you by circling a number. A 3 indicates a *strong* preference in that direction, 2 indicates a *moderate* preference in that direction, 1 indicates a *slight* preference in that direction, 0 indicates no preference in either direction/an equally strong preference in both directions.

I would like the therapist to...

1. Focus on specific goals			No or equal preference			Not focus on specific goals
3	2	1	0	-1	-2	-3

2. Give structure to the therapy			No or equal preference			Allow the therapy to be unstructured
3	2	1	0	-1	-2	-3

3. Teach me skills to deal with my problems			No or equal preference			Not teach me skills to deal with my problems
3	2	1	0	-1	-2	-3

4. Give me 'homework' to do		No or equal preference			Not give me 'homework' to do	
3	2	1	0	-1	-2	-3

5. Take a lead in therapy		No or equal preference			Allow me to take a lead in therapy	
3	2	1	0	-1	-2	-3

Scale 1. If score is 8 to 15 then strong preference for therapist directiveness. If score is -2 to 7 then no strong preference. If score is -3 to -15 then strong preference for client directiveness.

6. Encourage me to go into difficult emotions		No or equal preference			Not encourage me to go into difficult emotions	
3	2	1	0	-1	-2	-3

7. Talk with me about the therapy relationship		No or equal preference			Not talk with me about the therapy relationship	
3	2	1	0	-1	-2	-3

8. Focus on the relationship between us		No or equal preference			Not focus on the relationship between us	
3	2	1	0	-1	-2	-3

9. Encourage me to express strong feelings		No or equal preference			Not encourage me to express strong feelings	
3	2	1	0	-1	-2	-3

10. Focus mainly on my feelings		No or equal preference			Focus mainly on my thoughts	
3	2	1	0	-1	-2	-3

Scale 2. If score is 7 to 15 then strong preference for emotional intensity. If score is 0 to 6 then no strong preference. If score is -15 to-1 then strong preference for emotional reserve.

11. Focus on my life in the past		No or equal preference			Focus on my life in the present	
3	2	1	0	-1	-2	-3

12. Help me reflect on my childhood		No or equal preference			Help me reflect on my adulthood	
3	2	1	0	-1	-2	-3

13. Focus on my past		No or equal preference			Focus on my future	
3	2	1	0	-1	-2	-3

Scale 3. If score is 3 to 9 then strong preference for past orientation. If score is -2 to 2 then no strong preference. If score is -3 to -9 then strong preference for present orientation.

14. Be gentle		No or equal preference			Be challenging	
3	2	1	0	-1	-2	-3

15. Be supportive		No or equal preference			Be confrontational	
3	2	1	0	-1	-2	-3

16. Not interrupt me		No or equal preference			Interrupt me and keep me focused	
3	2	1	0	-1	-2	-3

17. Not be challenging of my own beliefs and views		No or equal preference			Be challenging of my own beliefs and views	
3	2	1	0	-1	-2	-3

18. Support my behaviour unconditionally		No or equal preference			Challenge my behaviour if they think it's wrong	
3	2	1	0	-1	-2	-3

> **Scale 4.** If score is 4 to 15 then strong preference for warm support. If score is -3 to 3 then no strong preference. If score is -4 to -15 then strong preference for focused challenge.

Additional client preferences for exploration and consideration (as appropriate to service provision).

Do you have a *strong* preference for:

- A therapist of a particular **gender**, **race/ethnicity**, **sexual orientation**, **religion**, or **other personal characteristic**?
- A therapist/counsellor who speaks a **specific language** that is most comfortable for you?
- **Modality** of therapy: such as individual, couple, family, or group therapy?
- **Orientation** of therapy: such as psychodynamic, cognitive, person-centred, or other?
- **Number** of therapy sessions: such as four, dependent on review, open-ended, or other?
- **Length** of therapy sessions: such as 50 mins, 60 mins, 90 mins or other?
- **Frequency** of therapy: such as twice weekly, weekly, monthly, ad hoc or other?
- **Medication**, psychotherapy, or both in combination?
- Use of **self-help** books, self-help groups, or computer programs in addition to therapy?
- **Any other** strong preferences that come to mind (and do raise them at any point in therapy)?
- What would you most **dislike** or **despise** happening in your therapy or counselling?

© licensed under the Creative Commons Attribution - Non-Commercial - No Derivatives 4.0 International (CCBY-NC-ND 4.0).

Glossary

CASE FORMULATION – the conceptualisation of a client's presentation that describes their experiences and events, gives some interpretation of the meaning of the events, and offers suggestions on how the therapy might progress. In pluralism, this formulation is always co-created between the client and therapist.

CHANGE PATHWAYS – the unique process of change that each client follows, according to their needs and preferences.

COLLABORATIVE RELATIONSHIP – the client and therapist working together with a shared purpose, using feedback and pooling knowledge and resources in therapy to achieve the best experience and outcome for the client.

COMMON FACTORS – aspects of therapy that lead to positive outcomes and are found in all therapy schools and modalities.

COUNSELLING SKILLS – the foundational skills that all therapists possess that allow them to create therapeutic relationships and deliver interventions.

ECLECTICISM – in therapy, the application of therapy methods that are appropriate for the client and deemed applicable to the presenting problem.

EXTRA-THERAPY RESOURCES – things that each person has available to them from their own socio-cultural context and networks that support or enhance their wellbeing.

GOALS, TASKS, METHODS – terms used for the domains of pluralistic therapy action. GOALS are the desired outcomes or purpose of the therapy for the client; TASKS are the activities that need to be done to reach the goal(s); METHODS are the what the client and therapist do to undertake the tasks.

HEROIC CLIENT – the understanding that it is the client who undertakes the challenges, faces the difficulties and ultimately makes the therapy work. Pluralistic therapists strive to enable and empower the client to do this.

HUMANISM – a philosophical stance that centres around the human capacity for self-knowledge and self-determination.

INTEGRATION – the practice of drawing on two or more schools or modalities of therapy within the same intervention or practice.

META-COMMUNICATION (OR META-THERAPEUTIC COMMUNICATION) – put simply, talking about what is going on; a way of observing therapy, making insights and comments about the process and interactions and inviting open feedback.

PLURALISM – a philosophical stance that accepts that there is no single 'truth'; rather, there are multiple and conflicting 'truths' Applied to counselling and psychotherapy, it describes the stance that there is no one true (and best) model of therapy.

PLURALISTIC FRAMEWORK – the framework of activities encompassed within the pluralistic approach for the practice of therapy. It includes guidelines on how a therapist might go about working pluralistically – for example, in developing a collaborative relationship, shared decision-making, case formulation and so forth.

PLURALISTIC PRACTICE – undertaken by a pluralistic therapist who aligns to the principles of the pluralistic approach.

PLURALISTIC STANCE – the belief that there are many effective ways of undertaking therapy and all have their place.

POSTMODERNISM – the philosophical stance that proposes that it is not possible to establish truth because all systems of understanding are embedded in their historical context.

PROBLEMS IN LIVING – a phrase used for any client difficulty presented in therapy.

RELATIONAL PLURALISM – the ways in which different relationship styles are used by therapists with different clients, and sometimes while working on different activities with the same client. It recognises that different methods and tasks may require therapists to adopt different relational and interactional styles.

SCHOOLISM – explicit alignment to one school or modality of therapy, to the exclusion of others.

SHARED DECISION-MAKING – the process of open discussion and information-sharing whereby both therapist and client are involved in decisions about and within therapy.

TASK LIST – a conceptual list of therapeutic activities that are commonly used for working with particular client presentations or experiences.

THERAPIST MENU – the collection of methods, activities, and interventions that a therapist can offer a client.

TIMELINE FORMULATION – a case formulation represented as a line from birth to the present day and into the future that depicts relevant aspects of the client's experience in the order in which they occurred. It can also include unique positive features of the client, their goals and links between events.

References

Antoniou, P., Cooper, M., Tempier, A. & Holliday, C. (2017). Helpful aspects of pluralistic therapy for depression. *Counselling and Psychotherapy Research, 17*(2), 137–147. https://doi.org/10.1002/capr.12116

Atcheson, S. (2018, November 30). Allyship – The key to unlocking the power of diversity. *Forbes.* http://www.forbes.com/sites/shereeatcheson/2018/11/30/allyship-the-key-to-unlocking-the-power-of-diversity/?sh=5a8eee7649c6

Barrett, M.S., Chua, W., Crits-Christoph, P., Gibbons, M.B. & Thompson, D. (2008). Early withdrawal from mental health treatment: Implications for psychotherapy practice. *Psychotherapy: Theory, research, practice, training, 45*(2), 247–267. https://doi.org/10.1037/0033-3204.45.2.247

Berger, T. (2017). The therapeutic alliance in internet interventions: A narrative review and suggestions for future research. *Psychotherapy Research, 27*(5), 511–524. https://doi.org/10.1080/10503307.2015.1119908

Beutler, L.E. & Consoli, A.J. (1993). Matching the therapist's interpersonal stance to clients' characteristics: Contributions from systematic eclectic psychotherapy. *Psychotherapy: Theory, research, practice, training, 30*(3), 417–422. https://doi.org/10.1037/0033-3204.30.3.417

Blunden, N. (2020, November 21). We're making it up as we go along! Co-production in pluralistic person-centred therapy. *Pluralistic Practice.* https://pluralisticpractice.com/2020/04/16/were-making-it-up-as-we-go-along-co-production-in-pluralistic-person-centred-therapy/

Bohart, A.C. & Tallman, K. (1999). *How clients make therapy work: The process of active self-healing.* American Psychological Association.

Bordin, E.S. (1979). The generalizability of the psychoanalytic concept of the working alliance. *Psychotherapy: Theory, research & practice, 16*(3), 252–260.

Bowen, M. & Cooper, M. (2012). Development of a client feedback tool: a qualitative study of therapists' experiences of using the Therapy Personalisation Form. *European Journal of Psychotherapy and Counselling, 14*(1), 47–62.

Brown, T. (2009). *Change by design: How design thinking transforms organizations and inspires innovation.* Harper Business.

Castonguay, L.G. & Hill, C.E. (2007). *Insight in psychotherapy* (1st ed.). American Psychological Association.

Cipolletta, S., Frassoni, E. & Faccio, E. (2018). Construing a therapeutic relationship online: An analysis of videoconference sessions. *Australian Psychological Society, 22*(2), 220–229. https://doi.org/10.1111/cp.12117

Cooper, M. (2008). *Essential research findings in counselling and psychotherapy: The facts are friendly.* Sage.

Cooper, M. (2016). Core counselling methods for pluralistic practice. In M. Cooper & W. Dryden (Eds.), *The Handbook of pluralistic counselling and psychotherapy* (pp.80–92). Sage.

Cooper, M. (2019). *Integrating counselling and psychotherapy: Directionality, synergy and social change.* Sage.

Cooper, M. & Dryden, W. (2016). *The handbook of pluralistic counselling and psychotherapy.* Sage.

Cooper, M., Dryden, W., Martin, K. & Papyianni, F. (2016). Metatherapeutic communication and shared decision-making. In M. Cooper & W. Dryden (Eds.), *The Handbook of pluralistic counselling and psychotherapy* (pp.42–53). Sage.

Cooper, M. & Law, D. (Eds.). (2018). *Working with goals in psychotherapy and counselling.* Oxford University Press.

Cooper, M. & McLeod, J. (2007). A pluralistic framework for counselling and psychotherapy: implications for research. *Counselling and Psychotherapy Research, 7*(3), 135–143.

Cooper, M. & McLeod, J. (2011a). *Pluralistic counselling and psychotherapy.* Sage.

Cooper, M. & McLeod, J. (2011b). Person-centered therapy: A pluralistic perspective. *Person-Centered & Experiential Psychotherapies, 10*(3), 210–223. https://doi.org/10.1080/14779757.2011.599517

Cooper, M. & Norcross, J.C. (2016). A brief, multidimensional measure of clients' therapy preferences: The Cooper-Norcross inventory of preferences (C-NIP). *International Journal of Clinical and Health Psychology, 16*(1), 87–98. https://doi.org/10.1016/j.ijchp.2015.08.003

Cooper, M., Norcross, J.C., Raymond-Barker, B. & Hogan, T.P. (2019). Psychotherapy preferences of laypersons and mental health professionals: Whose therapy is it? *Psychotherapy, 56*(2), 205–216. https://doi.org/10.1037/pst0000226

Cooper, M., Wild, C., van Rijn, B., Ward, T., McLeod, J., Cassar, S., Antonious P, Michael C., Michalitsi M, & Sreenath, S. (2015). Pluralistic therapy for depression: Acceptability, outcomes and helpful aspects in a multisite study. *Counselling Psychology Review, 30*(1), 6–20.

Creamer, M. & Timulak, L. (2016). Supervision in pluralistic counselling and psychotherapy. In M. Cooper & W. Dryden (Eds.), *The handbook of pluralistic counselling and psychotherapy* (pp.314–325). Sage.

Cummings, A.L., Martin, J., Hallberg, E. & Slemon, A. (1992). Memory for therapeutic events, session effectiveness, and working alliance in short-term counselling. *Journal of Counseling Psychology, 39*(3), 306–312. https://doi.org/10.1037//0022-0167.39.3.306

Curran, J., Parry, G.D., Hardy, G.E., Darling, J., Mason, A-M. & Chambers, E. (2019). How does therapy harm? A model of adverse process using task analysis in the meta-synthesis of service users' experience. *Frontiers in Psychology, 10,* 347. https://doi.org/10.3389/fpsyg.2019.00347

Dattilio, F.M. & Norcross, J.C. (2006). Psychotherapy integration end the emergence of instinctual territoriality. *Archives of Psychiatry and Psychotherapy, 8*(1), 5–16.

Davies, E. & Burdett J. (2004). Preventing 'schizophrenia': creating the conditions for saner societies. In J. Read, L.R. Mosher & R.P. Bentall (Eds.), *Models of Madness: Psychological, social and biogiocal approaches to schizophrenia* (pp. 271–282). Routledge.

de la Prida, A. (2020). *What works in counselling and psychotherapy.* BACP GPCP 004. British Association for Counselling and Psychotherapy.

Denzin, N.K. (2006). *Sociological methods: A sourcebook* (5th ed.). Aldine Transaction.

Denzin, N.K. (2012). Triangulation 2.0. *Journal of Mixed Methods Research, 6*(2), 80–88. https://doi.org/10.1177/1558689812437186

di Malta, G., Oddli, H.W. & Cooper, M. (2019). From intention to action: A mixed methods study of clients' experiences of goal-oriented practices. *Journal of Clinical Psychology, 75*(10), 1770–1789. https://doi.org/10.1002/jclp.22821

Duncan, B.L., Miller, S.D. & Sparks, J.A. (2004). *The heroic client: A revolutionary way to improve effectiveness through client-directed, outcome-informed therapy.* Wiley.

Duncan, B.L., Miller, S.D., Wampold, B.E. & Hubble, M.A. (2010). *The heart and soul of change: Delivering what works in therapy* (2nd ed.). American Psychological Association.

Eells, T.D. (2007). *Handbook of psychotherapy case formulation* (2nd ed.). Guilford Press.

Elliott, R. (1985). Helpful and nonhelpful events in brief counseling interviews: An empirical taxonomy. *Journal of Counseling Psychology, 32*(3), 307–322.

Eubanks, C.F., Burckell, L.A. & Goldfried, M.R. (2018). Clinical consensus strategies to repair ruptures in the therapeutic alliance. *Journal of Psychotherapy Integration, 28*(1), 60–76. https://doi.org/10.1037/int0000097

Evans, C., Mellor-Clark, J., Margison, F., Barkham, M., McGrath, G., Connell, J. & Audin, K. (2000). Clinical outcomes in routine evaluation: The CORE-OM. *Journal of Mental Health, 9*, 247–255.

Fernandez-Alvarez, H., Consoli, A.J. & Gomez, B. (2016). Integration in psychotherapy: Reasons and challenges. *American Psychologist, 71*(8), 820–830.

Finnerty, M., Kearns, C. & O'Regan, D. (2018). Pluralism: an ethical commitment to dialogue and collaboration. *Irish Journal of Counselling and Psychotherapy, 18*(3), 14–22.

Flückiger, C., Del Re, A.C., Wampold, B.E., Symonds, D. & Horvath, A.O. (2012). How central is the alliance in psychotherapy? A multilevel longitudinal meta-analysis. *Journal of Counseling Psychology, 59*(1), 10–17. https://doi.org/10.1037/a0025749

Freedman, J. & Combs, G. (1996). *Narrative therapy: the social construction of preferred realities.* W.W. Norton & Co.

Friedman, S. (1997). *The new language of change: Constructive collaboration in psychotherapy.* Guilford Press.

Gabriel, L. (2016). Ethics in pluralistic counselling and psychotherapy. In M. Cooper & W. Dryden (Eds.), *The handbook of pluralistic counselling and psychotherapy* (pp.300–313). Sage.

Gabriel, L. & Casemore, R. (Eds.). (2009). *Relational ethics in practice: Narratives from counselling and psychotherapy.* Routledge.

Geller, S. (2020). Cultivating online therapeutic presence: strengthening therapeutic relationships in teletherapy sessions. *Counselling Psychology Quarterly.* https://doi.org/10.1080/09515070.2020.1787348

Gibson, A., Cooper, M., Rae, J. & Hayes, J. (2020). Clients' experiences of shared decision-making in an integrative psychotherapy for depression. *Journal of Evaluation in Clinical Practice, 26*(2), 559–568. https://doi.org/10.1111/jep.13320

Greenberg, L. & Watson, J. (1998). Experiential therapy of depression: Differential effects of client-centered relationship conditions and process experiential interventions. *Psychotherapy Research, 8*(2), 210–224. https://doi.org/10.1080/10503309812331332317

Greenhalgh, T., Jackson, C., Shaw, S., & Janamian, T. (2016). Achieving research impact through co-creation in community-based health services: Literature review and case study. *The Milbank Quarterly, 94*(2), 392–429. doi: 10.1111/1468-0009.12197

Grosse Holtforth, M. & Grawe, K. (2002). Bern inventory of treatment goals: part 1. Development and first application of a taxonomy of treatment goal themes. *Psychotherapy Research, 12*(1), 79–99. https://doi.org/10.1093/ptr/12.1.79

Handelzalts, J.E. & Keinan, G. (2010). The effect of choice between test anxiety treatment options on treatment outcomes. *Psychotherapy Research, 20*(1), 100–112. https://doi.org/10.1080/10503300903121106

Hanley, T., Scott, A. & Winter, L.A. (2016). Humanistic approaches and pluralism. In M. Cooper & W. Dryden (Eds.), *The handbook of pluralistic counselling and psychotherapy* (pp.95–107). Sage.

Hanley, T. & Winter, L.A. (2016). Research and pluralistic counselling and psychotherapy. In M. Cooper & W. Dryden (Eds.), *The handbook of pluralistic counselling and psychotherapy* (pp.337–349). Sage.

Health Foundation (2013). *Implementing shared decision-making.* The Health Foundation.

Hill C.E., Castonguay, L.G., Farber, B.A., Knox, S., Stiles, W.B., Anderson, T., Angus, L.E., Barber, J.P., Gayle Beck, J., Bohart, A.C., Caspar, F., Constantino, M.J., ... Sharpless B.A. (2012). Corrective experiences in psychotherapy: Definitions, processes, consequences, and research directions. In L.G. Castonguay, C.E. Hill (Eds.), *Transformation in psychotherapy: Corrective experiences across cognitive-behavioral, humanistic, and psychodynamic approaches* (pp.355–370). APA Books.

Horvath, A.O., Del Re, A.C., Flückiger, C. & Symonds, D. (2011). Alliance in individual psychotherapy. *Psychotherapy, 48*(1), 9–16.

Johnstone, L. (2000). *Users and abusers of psychiatry: A critical look at psychiatric practice.* Routledge.

Johnstone, L. & Kopua, D. (2019). Crossing cultures with the Power Threat Meaning Framework. *Psychotherapy and Politics International, 17*(2). https://doi.org/10.1002/ppi.1494

Joosten, E.A.G., de Jong, C.A.J., de Weert-van Oene, G.H., Sensky, T. & van der Staak, C.P.F. (2009). Shared decision-making reduces drug use and psychiatric severity in substance-dependent patients. *Psychotherapy and Psychosomatics, 78*(4), 245–253. https://doi.org/10.1159/000219524

Kennedy-Moore, E. & Watson, J.C. (2001). *Expressing emotion: Myths, realities, and therapeutic strategies.* Guilford Press.

Klein, M.H., Mathieu-Coughlan, P., Kiesler, D.J., Pinsof, W.P. & Greenberg, L.S. (1986). *The psychotherapeutic process: A research handbook.* Guilford Press.

Kühnlein, I. (1999). Psychotherapy as a process of transformation: Analysis of posttherapeutic autobiographic narrations. *Psychotherapy Research, 9*(3), 274–287. https://doi.org/10.1080/10503309912331332761

Lambert, M.J. & Harmon, K.L. (2018). The merits of implementing routine outcome monitoring in clinical practice. *Clinical Psychology, 25*(4), e12268. https://doi.org/10.1111/cpsp.12268

Lambert, M.J. & Shimokawa, K. (2011). Collecting client feedback. *Psychotherapy, 48*(1), 72–79. https://doi.org/10.1037/a0022238

Lambert, M.J., Whipple, J.L., Smart, D.W., Vermeersch, D.A., Nielsen, S.L. & Hawkins, E.J. (2001). The effects of providing therapists with feedback on client progress during psychotherapy: Are outcomes enhanced? *Psychotherapy Research, 11*(1), 49–68.

Laska, K.M., Gurman, A.S. & Wampold, B.E. (2014). Expanding the lens of evidence-based practice in psychotherapy: A common factors perspective. *Psychotherapy, 51*(4), 467–481.

Lazarus, A.A. (1993). Tailoring the therapeutic relationship, or being an authentic chameleon. *Psychotherapy: Theory, research, practice, training, 30*(3), 404–407. https://doi.org/10.1037/0033-3204.30.3.404

Lazarus, A.A. & Beutler, L.E. (1993). On technical eclecticism. *Journal of Counselling and Development, 71*(4), 381–385.

Lazarus, A.A., Beutler, L.E. & Norcross, J.C. (1992). The future of technical eclecticism. *Psychotherapy, 29*(1), 11–20.

Lazarus, C.N. & Lazarus, A.A. (2019). Multimodal therapy. In J.C Norcross & M.R. Goldfried (Eds.), *Handbook of psychotherapy integration* (pp.125–140). Oxford University Press.

Levitt, H.M., Pomerville, A. & Surace, F.I. (2016). A qualitative meta-analysis examining clients' experiences of psychotherapy: A new agenda. *Psychological Bulletin, 142*(8), 801–830.

Lindhiem, O., Bennett, C.B., Trentacosta, C.J. & McLear, C. (2014). Client preferences affect treatment satisfaction, completion, and clinical outcome: A meta-analysis. *Clinical Psychology Review, 34*(6), 506–517. https://doi.org/10.1016/j.cpr.2014.06.002

Luborsky, L., Singer, B. & Luborsky, L. (1975). Comparative studies of psychotherapies: Is it true that 'Everyone has won and all must have prizes'? *Archives of General Psychiatry, 32*(8), 995–1008.

Mackrill, T. (2010). Goal consensus and collaboration in psychotherapy: An existential rationale. *The Journal of Humanistic Psychology, 50*(1), 96–107. https://doi.org/10.1177/0022167809341997

Martin, J. & Stelmaczonek, K. (1988). Participants' identification and recall of important events in counseling. *Journal of Counseling Psychology, 35*(4), 385–390. https://doi.org/10.1037/0022-0167.35.4.385

Marx, K. (1977). Economic and philosophic manuscripts of 1844. In D. McLelland (Ed.), *Karl Marx: Selected writings* (pp.95). Open University Press.

McLellan, G. (1995) *Pluralism*. Oxford University Press.

McLeod, J. (2012). What do clients want from therapy? A practice-friendly review of research into client preferences. *European Journal of Psychotherapy and Counselling, 14*(1), 19–32.

McLeod, J. (2013). Process and outcome in pluralistic Transactional Analysis counselling for long-term health conditions: A case series. *Counselling and Psychotherapy Research, 13*(1), 32–43. https://doi.org/10.1080/14733145.2012.709873

McLeod, J. (2018). *Pluralistic Therapy: Distinctive features* (1st ed.). Routledge.

McLeod, J. (2021). How students use deliberate practice during the first stage of counsellor training. *Counselling and Psychotherapy Research.* Advance online publication. https://doi.org/10.1002/capr.12397

McLeod, J. & McLeod, J. (2011). *Counselling skills: A practical guide for counsellors and helping professionals* (2nd ed.). Open University Press.

McLeod, J. & McLeod, J. (2016). Assessment and formulation in pluralistic counselling and psychotherapy. In M. Cooper & W. Dryden (Eds.), *The handbook of pluralistic counselling and psychotherapy* (pp.15–27). Sage.

McLeod, J., Smith, K. & Thurston, M. (2016). Training in pluralistic practice. In M. Cooper & W. Dryden (Eds.), *The handbook of pluralistic counselling and psychotherapy* (pp.326–336). Sage.

Miller, E. & Willig, C. (2012). Pluralistic counselling and HIV-positive clients: The importance of shared understanding. *European Journal of Psychotherapy & Counselling, 14*(1), 33–45. https://doi.org/10.1080/13642537.2012.652391

Muran, J.C. & Barber, J.P. (2010). *The therapeutic alliance: An evidence-based guide to practice.* Guilford Press.

Nilsson, T., Svensson, M., Sandell, R. & Clinton, D. (2007). Patients' experiences of change in cognitive-behavioral therapy and psychodynamic therapy: A qualitative comparative study. *Psychotherapy Research, 17*(5), 553–566. https://doi.org/10.1080/10503300601139988

Norcross, J.C. (2011). *Psychotherapy relationships that work: Evidence-based responsiveness.* Oxford University Press.

Norcross, J.C. & Alexander, E.F. (2019). A primer on psychotherapy integration. In J.C. Norcross & M.R. Goldfried (2019), *Handbook of psychotherapy integration* (3rd ed., pp.3–27). Oxford University Press.

Norcross, J.C. & Lambert, M.J. (Eds.). (2019). *Psychotherapy relationships that work* (Vol. 1, 3rd ed.). Oxford University Press.

Norcross, J.C. & Wampold, B.E. (2018). A new therapy for each patient: Evidence-based relationships and responsiveness. *Journal of Clinical Psychology, 74*(11), 1889–1906. https://doi.org/10.1002/jclp.22678

Oddli, H.W. & Rønnestad, M.H. (2012). How experienced therapists introduce the technical aspects in the initial alliance formation: Powerful decision makers supporting clients' agency. *Psychotherapy Research, 22*(2), 176–193. https://doi.org/10.1080/10503307.2011.633280

Ong, W.T., Murphy, D. & Joseph, S. (2020). Unnecessary and incompatible: A critical response to Cooper and McLeod's conceptualization of a pluralistic framework for person-centered therapy. *Person-Centered & Experiential Psychotherapies, 19*(2), 168–182. https://doi.org/10.1080/14779757.2020.1717987

Parsons, A., Omylinska-Thurston, J., Karkou, V., Harlow, J., Haslam, S., Hobson, J., Nair, K., Dubrow-Marshall, L., Thurston, S. & Griffin, J. (2020). Arts for the blues – a new creative psychological therapy for depression. *British Journal of Guidance & Counselling, 48*(1), 5–20. https://doi.org/10.1080/03069885.2019.1633459

Parsons, A., Turner, R., Ingleton, H., Dubrow-Marshall, L., Kefalogianni, M., Omylinska-Thurston, J., Karkou, V. & Thurston, S. (2021). Flowing towards freedom with multimodal creative therapy: The healing power of therapeutic arts for ex-cult members. *The Arts in Psychotherapy, 72*, 101743. https://doi.org/10.1016/j.aip.2020.101743

Perren, S., Godfrey, M. & Rowland, N. (2009). The long-term effects of counselling: The process and mechanisms that contribute to ongoing change from a user perspective. *Counselling and Psychotherapy Research, 9*(4), 241–249. https://doi.org/10.1080/14733140903150745

Prochaska, J.O. & DiClemente, C.C. (1982). Transtheoretical therapy: Toward a more integrative model of change. *Psychotherapy: Theory, research & practice, 19*(3), 276–288.

Prochaska, J.O. & Norcross, J.C. (2018). *Systems of psychotherapy: A transtheoretical analysis* (9th ed.). Oxford University Press.

Rennie, D.L. (1994). Clients' deference in psychotherapy. *Journal of Counseling Psychology, 41*(4), 427–437.

Rescher, N. (1993). *Pluralism against the demand for consensus*. Clarendon Press.

Rousmaniere, T. (2016). *Deliberate practice for psychotherapists: A guide to improving clinical effectiveness*. Routledge.

Safran, J.D. & Muran, J.C. (2006). Has the concept of the therapeutic alliance outlived its usefulness? *Psychotherapy: Theory, research, practice, training, 43*(3), 286–291.

Schmid, P. F. (2001). Acknowledgement: The art of responding. Dialogical and ethical perspectives on the challenge of unconditional personal relationships in therapy and beyond. In J. Bozarth & P. Wilkins (Eds.), *Unconditional positive regard* (pp.155–171). PCCS Books.

Silverstone, L. (1997). *Art therapy – The person-centred way: Art and the development of the person* (2nd ed.). Jessica Kingsley.

Skovholt, T. & Jennings, L. (2005). Mastery and expertise in counselling. *Journal of Mental Health Counseling, 27*(1), 13–18. https://doi.org/10.17744/mehc.27.1.gnblmy6g3dbqduq4

Smith, K., Thurston, M. & Eva, P. (In press). Relational pluralism: adjusting according to task in pluralism. *Counselling and Psychotherapy Research*.

Sparks, J.A. & Duncan, B.L. (2016). Client strengths and resources: Helping clients draw on what they do best. In M. Cooper & W. Dryden (Eds.), *The handbook of pluralistic counselling and psychotherapy* (pp.68–79). Sage.

Springham, N. (2008). Through the eyes of the law: What is it about art that can harm people? *International Journal of Art Therapy, 13*, 65–73. https://doi.org/10.1080/17454830802489141

Spurling, L. (2016). Psychodynamic approaches and pluralism. In M. Cooper & W. Dryden (Eds.), *The handbook of pluralistic counselling and psychotherapy* (pp.122–133). Sage.

Stiles, W.B., Elliott, R., Llewelyn, S.P., Firth-Cozens, J., Margison, F.R., Shapiro, D.A. & Hardy, G. (1990). Assimilation of problematic experiences by clients in psychotherapy. *Psychotherapy; Theory, research, practice, training, 27*(3), 411–420. https://doi.org/10.1037/0033-3204.27.3.411

Stoll, M. & McLeod, J. (2019). A pluralistic approach to student counselling. *University and College Counselling, 7*(1), 4–11.

Stuckey, H.L. & Nobel, J. (2010). The connection between art, healing, and public health: A review of current literature. *American Journal of Public Health, 100*(2), 254–263. https://doi.org/10.2105/AJPH.2008.156497

Suler, J. (2005). The online disinhibition effect. *International Journal of Applied Psychoanalytic Studies, 2*(2), 184–188. https://doi.org/10.1002/aps.42

Swift, J.K., Callahan, J.L., Cooper, M. & Parkin, S.R. (2018). The impact of accommodating client preference in psychotherapy: A meta-analysis. *Journal of Clinical Psychology, 74*(11), 1924–1937. https://doi.org/10.1002/jclp.22680

Swift, J.K. & Greenberg, R.P. (2015). *Premature termination in psychotherapy: Strategies for engaging clients and improving outcomes.* American Psychological Association.

Swift, J.K. & Parkin, S.R. (2017). The client as the expert in psychotherapy: What clinicians and researchers can learn about treatment processes and outcomes from psychotherapy clients. *Journal of Clinical Psychology, 73*(11), 1486–1488. https://doi.org/10.1002/jclp.22528

Thoma, N.C. & Cecero, J.J. (2009). Is integrative use of techniques in psychotherapy the exception or the rule? Results of a national survey of doctoral-level practitioners. *Psychotherapy, 46*(4), 405–417. https://doi.org/10.1037/a0017900

Thompson, A., Cooper, M. & Pauli, R. (2017). Development of a therapists' self-report measure of pluralistic thought and practice: The therapy pluralism inventory. *British Journal of Guidance & Counselling, 45*(5), 489–499. https://doi.org/10.1080/03069885.2017.1373745

Thurston, M. (2016). *Emotional support and inclusion for blind and partially sighted people in the United Kingdom: The development of counselling for sight loss, a pluralistic practice model.* Doctoral thesis. Abertay University.

Timulak, L. (2010). Significant events in psychotherapy: An update of research findings. *Psychology & Psychotherapy, 83*(4), 421–447. https://doi.org/10.1348/147608310x499404

Tryon, G.S. & Winograd, G. (2011). Goal consensus and collaboration. *Psychotherapy, 48*(1), 50–57.

Utry, Z.A., Palmer, S., McLeod, J. & Cooper, M. (2015). A pluralistic approach to coaching. *The Coaching Psychologist, 11*(1), 46–52.

Vermeulen, T. & van den Akker, R. (2010). Notes on metamodernism. *Journal of Aesthetics & Culture, 2*(1), 5677. https://doi.org/10.3402/jac.v2i0.5677

Wachtel, P.L. (2014). An integrative relational point of view. *Psychotherapy, 51*(3), 342–349. https://doi.org/10.1037/a0037219

Wakefield, J.C., Baer, J.C. & Conrad, J.A. (2020). Levels of meaning and the need for psychotherapy integration. *Clinical Social Work Journal, 48*(3), 236–256. https://doi.org/10.1007/s10615-020-00769-6

Walls, J., McLeod, J., & McLeod, J. (2016). Client preferences in counselling for alcohol problems: A qualitative investigation. *Counselling and Psychotherapy Research, 16*(2), 109–118.

Watson, V.C., Cooper, M., McArthur, K. & McLeod, J. (2012). Helpful therapeutic processes: Client activities, therapist activities and helpful effects. *European Journal of Psychotherapy & Counselling, 14*(1), 77–89. https://doi.org/10.1080/13642537.2012.652395

White, M. & Epston D. (1990). *Narrative means to therapeutic ends.* W.W. Norton & Co.

Winter, L.A., Feng, G., Katarzyna, W. & Hanley, T. (2016). Difference and diversity in pluralistic counselling and psychotherapy. In M. Cooper & W. Dryden (Eds.), *The handbook of pluralistic counselling and psychotherapy* (pp.275–287). Sage.

Zarbo, C., Tasca, G.A., Cattafi, F. & Compare, A. (2016). Integrative psychotherapy works. *Frontiers in Psychology 6*, 2021. https://doi.org/10.3389/fpsyg.2015.02021

Index

A

adaptation
    communication, 35–36
    relational, 32–33
    therapist, 17, 74–75
Albee, G.W. 5
Alexander, E.F. 9
Antoniou, P. 82
Atcheson, S. 66

B

Barber, J.P. 25
Barrett, M.S. 40
Berger, T. 25, 80
Beutler, L.E. 11, 31
black box 26
Blunden, N. 29
Bohart, A.C. 23, 81
Bordin, E.S. 25
Bowen, M. 58, 83
Brown, T. 28
Buber, M. x
Burdett, J. 5

C

caring 13
Casemore, R. 14
Castonguay, L.G. 60
Cecero, J.J. 54
CASE FORMULATION
    difficulties 72
    early stages of, 42–44
    examples of, 61–62
    steps to, 43
change
    collaboration 18–19, 31-4
    goals 2, 24, 32, 40, 46–47
    pathways 61–62
    process 8, 11, 29, 46, 59–60, 98
    therapeutic, 15, 17, 25, 64
    structural, 5, 68
Cipolletta, S. 80
collaboration 29–36, 42, 47, 70–75, 82–87
Combs, G. 35
Consoli, A.J. 31
constructionism 35
co-creation 19, 86, 91
Cooper, M. 8, 9–10, 13, 14, 15, 16, 17, 18, 19, 28, 36, 45, 46, 49, 51, 53, 56, 58, 60, 62–63, 67–68, 75, 76, 77, 82, 83, 85, 94
Creamer, M. 69
cultural resources 24, 56
Cummings, A.L. 82
Curran, J. 18

D

Datillio, F.M. 8
Davies, E. 5
de la Prida, A. 25, 63

decision-making
 ethical, 65
 and meta-communication 36–38
 risk 94
 shared, 19, 26–30
Denzin, N.K. 86
DiClemente, C.C. 11
di Malta, G. 45, 46, 47
diversity
 of perspectives 29–30
 recognition of, 14–15, 77
Dryden, W. 16, 19, 62–63, 77
Duncan, B.L. 14, 23, 25, 26

E

Eells, T.D. 42
Elliott, R. 82
emotion
 distress 2–3
 -focused therapy 50–51
 process 32–33, 47, 60
 response 28, 90–91
empathy 16, 19, 67
Epston, D. 35
equality 15, 18, 87–88
ethics/ethical
 adaptation 17
 collaboration 18, 82
 decision-making 65
 individuality 11
 integration 10, 75
 principles 7, 13–14, 76
Eubanks, C.F. 34
Evans, C. 94
EXTRA-THERAPY RESOURCES (*see also* cultural resources) 41, 57, 61–62, 79, 83, 100

F

feedback 35–37, 54, 57–58

 client, 76, 80, 85
 supervision, 70
 systems 81–83, 94
Fernandez-Alvarez, H. 9
Finnerty, M. 10
flexibility
 client, 100–102
 therapeutic, 19, 35, 77
 therapist, 17–18, 54, 81
Flückiger, C. 25
Freedman, J. 35

G

Gabriel, L. 14, 187
Geller, S. 80
Gibson, A. 37
GOALS
 client, 8, 23, 44, 47–48, 87
 group-based, 80
 progress 57–59
 therapy, 45–46, 70–71, 82, 91
 understanding 40
Goldfried, M.R. 11
Grawe, K. 45
Greenberg, L. 45
Greenberg, R.P. 40
Greenhalgh, T. 86
Grosse Holtforth, M. 45

H

Handelzalts, J.E. 82
Hanley, T. 45, 85
Harmon, K.L. 45, 57
Health Foundation 82
heroic client 23–25, 75
Hill, C.E. 60
hope 28, 40
Horvath, A.O. 25, 82

I

INTEGRATION 7, 11–12, 75–76

J

Jennings, L. 73
Johnstone, L. 22
Joosten, E.A.G. 82

K

Keinan, G. 82
Kennedy-Moore, E. 43
Klein, M.H. 45
knowledge
  client personal, 16, 27
  common 16, 27–28
  self-, 8, 18, 47, 59
  sub-conscious, 59
  personal, 61–62, 77
  theoretical, 43
  therapist, 17, 26–28
Kopua, D. 22
Kühnlein, I. 82

L

Lambert, M.J. 18, 28, 45, 57, 82
Laska, K.M. 11
Law, D. 45
Lazarus, A.A. 9, 11, 31
Lazarus, C.N. 9
Levitt, H.M. 60
Lindhiem, O. 82
Luborsky, L. 9

M

Mackrill, T. 45
Martin, J. 82
Marx, K. 8
McLellan, G. 8
McLeod, John xi, 8, 9–10, 11, 14, 15, 17, 18, 28, 42, 49, 54, 56, 60, 67–68, 73, 75, 76, 82, 83, 84, 85
McLeod, Julia 17, 42, 54
META-COMMUNICATION 28, 36–37, 41
metamodernism 8
Miller, E. 84
Muran, J.C. 11, 25
multiplicity 8, 11–12, 15, 69

N

Nilsson, T. 34, 42
Nobel, J. 79
Norcross, J.C. 8, 9, 11, 17, 18, 25, 26, 28, 58, 94

O

Oddli, H.W. 26, 27
Ong, W.T. 75
Other, the 13, 15

P

Parkin, S.R. 60
Parsons, A. 79
Perren, S. 82
person-centred therapy 43, 50–51, 64, 75
personal growth 5, 73
PLURALISTIC
  FRAMEWORK 67, 71
  STANCE 10, 14, 66, 74
primacy 14–15, 66, 75, 89
PROBLEMS IN LIVING 20–21
Prochaska, J.O. 8, 11

R

reflexivity 18–19, 67
relational pluralism 31–32
Rennie, D.L. 58, 82
Rescher, N. 8
responsiveness
  client 79, 84
  therapeutic 18–19, 59, 71, 76
Rønnestad, M.H. 26, 27

Rousmaniere, T. 73
ruptures
   addressing 33–34
   creation of, 19, 28, 63
   repairing, 63

S

Safran, J.D. 11
Schmid, P.E. 17, 35
SCHOOLISM 9–10, 14
Shimokawa, K.L. 82
Silverstone, L. 79
Skovholt, T. 73
Smith, K. 31
Sparks, J.A. 23
Springham, N. 79
Spurling, L. 74
Stelmaczonek, K. 82
Stiles, W.B. 11
Stoll, M. 9
Stuckey, H.L. 79
Suler, J. 35
supervision 69–73
Swift, J.K. 40, 60, 82

T

Tallman, K. 23, 81
task
   framework 79–80
   lists 49
   taxonomy 47–52
   therapeutic, 37, 41–45, 87
therapeutic alliance 25–26
Thoma, N.C. 54
Thompson, A. 10
Thurston, M. 85
TIMELINE 43, 93
Timulak, L. 69, 82
training
   values 12
   client 46

cultural, 14
pluralistic, 15, 69
professional, 67, 71
Trynon, G.S. 82

U

Utry, Z.A. 85

V

van den Akker, R. 8
Vermeulan, T. 8

W

Wachtel, P.L. 11
Wakefield, J.C. 10
Walls, J. 83
Wampold, B.E. 17, 26
Watson, J. 43, 45
Watson, V.C. 83
White, M. 35
Willig, C. 84
Winograd, G. 82
Winter, L.A. 24, 85

Z

Zarbo, C. 10

The Primers in Counselling Series by PCCS Books

This best-selling series offers comprehensive descriptions of key counselling approaches and contexts in the 21st century. Accessible and concise, they are ideal for students seeking a theory bridge between introductory, intermediate and diploma courses or for comparative essays and integrative theory assignments.

The other primers in the series are:

The Single-Session Counselling Primer – Windy Dryden
pbk 9781910919569 – epub 9781910919583

The Existential Counselling Primer (2nd edition) – Mick Cooper
pbk 9781910919750 – epub 9781910919767

The Person-Centred Counselling Primer – Pete Sanders
pbk 9781898059806 – epub 9781906254841

The Integrative Counselling Primer – Richard Worsley
pbk 9781898059813 – epub 9781906254902

The Experiential Counselling Primer – Nick Baker
pbk 9781898059837

The Contact Work Primer: Introduction to pre-therapy – edited by Pete Sanders   pbk 9781898059844

The Focusing-Oriented Counselling Primer (2nd edition) – Campbell Purton pbk 9781915220004 – epub 9781915220011

The Psychodynamic Counselling Primer – Mavis Klein
pbk 9781898059851 – epub 9781906254896

The Cognitive Behavioural Therapy Primer (2nd edition) – Rhena Branch, Jodie Paget and Windy Dryden
pbk 9781910919989 – epub 9781910919996

The Rational Emotive Behaviour Therapy Primer – Windy Dryden
pbk 9781910919965 – epub 9781910919972